Memories

of

Cambridge

Part of the

Memories

series

*The Publishers would like to thank the following companies for supporting
the production of this book*

Main Sponsor

Cambridge Regional College

Arundel House Hotel

Cambridge Building Society

Cambridge University Press

RG Carter Cambridge

Cecil Instruments Limited

Coulson Group Limited

Grant Instruments (Cambridge) Limited

Histon Tyre Service Limited

Ivett & Reed Limited

Kidman & Sons Limited

Korten Limited

George Lister & Sons

Ridgeons Limited

Herbert Robinson Limited

Simoco International Limited

Shelford Energy

First published in Great Britain by True North Books Limited
Units 3 - 5 Heathfield Industrial Park
Elland West Yorkshire
HX5 9AE
Tel. 01422 377977
© Copyright: True North Books Limited 1999

ISBN 1 900463 88 1

Text, design and origination by True North Books Limited
Printed and bound by The Amadeus Press Limited

Memories are made of this

Memories. We all have them; some good, some bad, but our memories of the city we grew up in are usually tucked away in a very special place in our minds. The best are usually connected with our childhood and youth, when we longed to be grown up and paid no attention to adults who told us to enjoy being young, as these were the best years of our lives. We look back now and realise that they were right.

So many memories - perhaps of the war and rationing, perhaps of parades, celebrations and Royal visits. And so many changes; one-way traffic systems and pedestrianisation. New trends in shopping led that to the very first self-serve stores being opened.

Through the bad times and the good, however, Cambridge not only survived but prospered. We have only to look at the city as it is today, with its finest buildings restored to their full glory, and the traditional tourist attractions now complemented by up-to-the-minute facilities, to see what progress has been realised and what achievements have been made over the last 50 years. Cambridge has a history to be proud of - but more importantly, a great future to look forward to, into the new millennium and beyond.

Contents

Around the city centre

This view of Bridge Street will take our more mature readers on a trip down Memory Lane. Looking north from the junction of Round Church Street, the block of buildings on the left which once housed the Singer sewing machine shop, Shallini (who specialised in lingerie), Darkins' Newsagents and Langdons builders and decorators, has long gone; in fact when this photograph was taken in 1937 the row of properties had only one year of life left to it before it was demolished. It was replaced by the building we are familiar with today, St John's Music School and accommodation block. Allin's Garage on the right, where you could not only buy a good second hand cycle but buy spares and accessories for your car and fill it up with Shell, BP or National petrol, were AA and RAC agents. Today you can 'curl up and dye' at the hairdresser's that has replaced Allin's cycle shop.

Events of the 1930s

HOT OFF THE PRESS

The years of the 1930s saw Adolf Hitler's sickening anti-Jewish campaign echoed in the streets of Britain. On 19th October 1936 Oswald Mosley's 7,000-strong British Union of Fascists clashed head on with thousands of Jews and Communists in London, resulting in 80 people being injured in the ensuing battle. Mosley and his 'blackshirts' later rampaged through the streets beating up Jews and smashing the windows of their businesses.

GETTING AROUND

At the beginning of the decade many believed that the airship was the transport of the future. The R101 airship, however, loaded with thousands of cubic metres of hydrogen, crashed in France on its maiden flight in 1930. Forty-eight passengers and crew lost their lives. In 1937 the Hindenburg burst into flames - the entire disaster caught on camera and described by a distraught reporter. The days of the airship were numbered.

SPORTING CHANCE

In 1939 British racing driver Sir Malcolm Campbell hit the headlines when he captured the world's water-speed record for the third time in 'Bluebird' - all his cars were given the same name. A racing driver who set world speed records both on land and on water, Sir Malcolm established world land-speed records no fewer than nine times. His son Donald went on to set further records, tragically dying in 1967 when his speedboat - also named 'Bluebird' - crashed.

Traffic at the junction of Sidney Street and Petty Cury seems virtually non existent in this photograph, so a passer-by appears to be taking advantage of the situation to ask for directions. The small drama is set against the background of a part of Cambridge that has seen vast changes in recent years. Since 1938, the date of the photograph, John Kittridge's

tobacconist's shop, Warrington & Sons' butcher's and Turner & Sons chemists and opticians business closed their doors for the last time to make way for the extensions to Boots.

Today we rarely see the 'traffic bobby' who were stationed at every major junction to control the flow of vehicles through city centres across the UK. The narrow streets of Cambridge were quite unsuited to the volume of traffic that built up over the years, leading to a ban on cars in the city centre between certain hours during the week, and park and ride schemes today provide motorists with an alternative.

Both pictures: A quiet day in the market - or is this the end of the day's trading? If so, it might be the ideal time to take the opportunity to snap up perishables that had been reduced by threepence or more.... Looking down on to the market from the end of Petty Cury, this scene was caught on camera in the late 1940s. Local housewives, who love a bargain as much as anyone else, would have made a beeline for the market. Its well-stocked fruit stalls would have been the first port of call for many, where a good selection of apples, pears, oranges, grapefruit and bananas was on offer. Apart from the gaily striped canvas of today, similar bargains are still to be had in the market, and not merely for fruit and vegetables.

Fashion for all the family, books, candles, rugs, Indian silk scarves - you name it and you can probably buy it in Cambridge Market, encouraged by the fact that the prices charged by street traders have traditionally been a few coppers cheaper than the larger high street shops would charge.

Many readers will remember the fountain as it was in the early 1950s, and this view *(above)* will give them a trip down Memory Lane. The fountain was built in the mid 19th century, and the intervening 100 years had taken their toll on the structure. Sadly, the top became unsafe and was removed in 1953, giving us the cropped version that we know today.

Both pictures: Even close inspection fails to reveal an exact date for these two photographs of Market Street and Sidney Street taken from the same spot, but the hairstyles, the knee length fashions worn by the ladies, the short trousers of the small boy - and the military uniform worn by the rather laid-back cyclist who isn't going anywhere in a hurry - all point to the second world war. We know that both photographs were almost certainly taken on the same day, as each view shows the same banner spanning Sidney Street. The banner itself is rather enigmatic, as all that can be read is 'Don't Chance it', leaving us, fifty-odd years on, to wonder what these passers-by should not take a chance on. Leaving their gas masks at home, perhaps? Or taking care not to get run over in the blackout? The large and stately Wolseley pictured here would have been one vehicle to avoid tangling with.... The weather was fine and sunny when these pictures were recorded, and the blinds are down above Joshua Taylor's window to protect the goods on display from the strong sunlight. J O Vinter & Son Ltd, who occupied the adjoining premises, were coal and coke merchants; the vast majority of households had open fires at the time, which burnt one or the other. They would perhaps not be doing too well at this particular time, however, as summer time would obviously be their slack period. Still, the cooler days of autumn lay just ahead, and business would soon be booming once more.

The vast majority of households in the 1940s had open fires

This was Petty Cury in May 1950; doesn't it seem strange to see lines of cars in the city centre? The photographer has captured a sight which will bring the memories flooding back to locals who remember Cambridge before the developers gave us the Lion Yard Complex....Burton's menswear on the corner of Market Hill and Petty Cury, with the Corner House Cafe above. How many of our readers have enjoyed

afternoon tea here, gazing down at the life and bustle of the market from one of these windows?

The sun blinds are down above the side windows of Burtons to protect their display from the glare. Montague Burton's good quality menswear has been a firm favourite with gentlemen for many years, and virtually every town and city in Britain has at least one branch. The story goes that when

Events of the 1930s

SCIENCE AND DISCOVERY
By observing the heavens, astronomers had long believed that there in the constellation of Gemini lay a new planet, so far undiscovered. They began to search for the elusive planet, and a special astronomical camera was built for the purpose. The planet Pluto was discovered by amateur astronomer Clyde Tombaugh in 1930, less than a year later.

WHAT'S ON?
In this heyday of the cinema, horrified audiences were left gasping at the sight of Fay Wray in the clutches of the giant ape in the film 'King Kong', released in 1933. Very different but just as gripping was the gutsy 1939 American Civil War romance 'Gone with the Wind'. Gable's parting words, 'Frankly, my dear, I don't give a damn' went down in history. 1936 - Britain set up the world's first television service - black and white, of course. The Queen's coronation in 1953, the first such ceremony to be televised, did much to popularise television.

ROYAL WATCH
The talking point of the early 1930s was the affair of the Prince of Wales, who later became King Edward VIII, and American divorcee Wallis Simpson. Faced with a choice, Edward gave up his throne for 'the woman I love' and spent the remainder of his life in exile. Many supported him, though they might not have been as keen to do so if they had been aware of his Nazi sympathies, kept strictly under wraps at the time.

soldiers were demobbed after military service they were given vouchers to be outfitted at Burtons. They went along to the nearest branch and were kitted out in what was termed 'the full Monty' - a phrase which has in recent years come to mean something very different from a full suit of clothes! Next door to Burtons was the International Stores, provision merchants; self service shopping was to sound the death knell for many small grocers over the next couple of decades.

Above: It was a busy day in Sidney Street when this scene was captured for posterity, and it is interesting to note that bicycles outnumber cars by around fifty to one! The scene has changed little today apart from a change to such names as 'Nine West', 'Costa' and 'Monsoon', which have replaced the names that were familiar to an earlier generation. Lloyds Bank still dominates the right of the scene, the legend in stone above the doorway interestingly informing passers by that this is the premises of 'Fosters Bank'. Marks and Spencer have of course extended their operations since the date of this photograph, and today occupy the property adjoining the bank as well as their traditional site.

Local people as well as visitors to the city will appreciate a recent addition to Sidney Street. Just off-picture to the left in Lion Yard is the church of St Andrew the Great and its churchyard, a scene transformed by the City Wildlife Group, who planted a wild flower garden there to delight the eye of passers by and cyclists who pause to chain their bicycles to the railings.

Above right: Heffers book shop, founded by William Heffer in Fitzroy Street back in 1876, was probably the most well known store in Petty Cury. Heffer opened a second shop in Petty Cury twenty years later - a shop that was to become beloved by students who enjoyed browsing among the books. Many readers will remember the shop's frontage of Dutch brick, bronze and frosted glass, the fine gallery and oak room and the nicely refitted upper floors - all sacrificed in the name of progress in the early 1970s. Heffers is still a well known name in the city, today trading from their shop in Trinity Street.

Steady rain was falling when this scene was recorded some time in the 1950s, and the wet roadway reflects the street lighting and the line of cars along Petty Cury. Classic car enthusiasts will immediately spot the Morris Minor, interestingly the first all-British car to sell more than one million. Developed by designer Alexander Issigonis, who also gave us the Mini, this tough little car has remained popular and is today attracting quite a following.

Below: It's August 1971 (rather cool, judging by the warm clothing worn in this photograph), and double yellow lines have made their appearance in Sidney Street - today one of the city's many car free areas. Also typical of the day are the cars that feature in the photograph, and the Cortina Mk 1, identified by its 'ban the bomb' tail lights, is worthy of a mention. The forerunner of the Mondeo and the Sierra, the Cortina was one of the first 'rep's express' cars, the object of every salesman's dream. Those were the days before electric demisting panels were common; note the plastic panel in the rear window that helped to keep

the glass from misting over. The car bears a Peterborough and Huntingdon registration, and interestingly, a GB plate which informs us that the car has explored foreign shores. The car in front is the universally beloved VW Beetle, which still enjoys wide popularity today.

Bottom: An old Nestle's Milk advert adds its own flavour to this view of Sidney Street - a view that will be unfamiliar to younger readers whose memories of the city go back no further than the redevelopment of Lion Yard and Petty Cury. Behind the delivery van on the right we can just make out

Kittridge's tobacconist's shop, which was one of those marvellous old traditional establishments, appropriately named 'The Noted Pipe House'. Kittridge's had displays of pipes of all makes and sizes, and a window filled with everything a smoker could ever need. Those, of course, were the days before smoking was linked with ill health, and just about every second person was a smoker. The tobacconist's was demolished along with the two adjoining properties to allow for extensions to Boots the Chemists, who were first established in Cambridge in the late 19th century. A recent addition to the scene is the pleasant garden of wild flowers that takes up a corner of the churchyard of St Andrew the Great, to the left of the photograph.

Isn't it strange how you can take for granted something that is with you for years, and only realise how much you appreciated it when it is gone? The flower seller whose stall was a riot of colour outside the Lion Hotel was like that. Sadly gone today, though not forgotten. Taken around 1960, this view of Petty Cury in the days before the Lion Yard Centre will bring back many memories.

Redevelopment of the area was on the cards as early as 1950, though it was 1968 before the design of the present development was accepted. At the time, the shops and services centred around Petty Cury were the life and soul of the city, offering everything from restaurants and night life to boutiques and greengrocery. When the south side of Petty Cury was demolished in 1972, Cambridge lost for

Events of the 1930s

MELODY MAKERS
Throughout the 1930s a young American trombonist called Glenn Miller was making his mark in the world of music. By 1939 the Glenn Miller sound was a clear leader in the field; his clean-cut, meticulously executed arrangements of numbers such as 'A String of Pearls' and 'Moonlight Serenade' brought him fame across the world as a big-band leader. During a flight to England from Paris in 1944 Miller's plane disappeared; no wreckage was ever found.

THE WORLD AT LARGE
In India, Gandhi's peaceful protests against British rule were gathering momentum. The Salt Laws were a great bone of contention: forced to buy salt from the British government, thousands of protestors marched to the salt works, intending to take it over in the name of the Indian people. Policemen and guards attacked the marchers, but not one of them fought back. Gandhi, who earned for himself the name 'Mahatma' - Great Soul - was assassinated in 1948.

INVENTION AND TECHNOLOGY
With no driving tests or speed restrictions, 120,000 people were killed on the roads in Britain between the two world wars. In 1934 a Halifax man, Percy Shaw, invented a safety device destined to become familiar the world over: reflecting roadstuds. In dark or foggy conditions the studs that reflected light from the car's headlights kept traffic on the 'straight and narrow' and must over the years have saved many lives.

ever many of its most important buildings - a loss that continues to be felt today. The Red Lion was an old coaching inn which by 1900 was flourishing. It was extended east to the rear of the shops in Petty Cury in 1903, the extension linked to the main hotel by a corridor at first floor level, lit by impressive stained glass windows. By the early 1970s the buildings on the right of the photograph had all been demolished to be replaced by the new shopping complex.

In the mid 1960s Laurie & McConnal's was a popular place to shop; the well-known department store, however, held a mystery: the bandstand on the roof. How many of our readers ever actually heard a band play from there? And why did the company have it built in the first place? This was surely the draughtiest bandstand in the UK! Vast changes, however, were to take place a few years down the line when Laurie & McConnal's, along with Peaks Furnishers next door (where many a Cambridge couple purchased carpets for their first home),

Laurie & McConnal's disappeared to make room for the Grafton Centre

closed and were eventually replaced by the Grafton Centre, Cambridge's newest shopping complex; today we would see Habitat from this particular viewpoint. Though Cambridge had its casualties such as Fitzroy Street and Petty Cury, the city escaped the wholesale destruction suffered by many cities across Britain in the 1960s and 70s, when an epidemic of reconstruction fever gripped the nation's planners. Today, the phrase 'the oldest shopping street in the city' is a matter for pride rather than a humiliation, though we have learned to live with and even appreciate the Grafton Centre and Lion Yard.

At leisure

Above: How many readers remember pleasant evenings spent at the Regal Cinema? The photograph shows the projection room as it was in July 1948, with the projectionists proudly standing alongside their equipment. The management of the Regal believed in presenting their audiences with clear and well defined pictures, and early in the theatre's life they installed Ross kinematograph projectors and lamps, which had earned a good reputation as being among the finest equipment in the world, for their performance as well as their mechanical superiority. Sound reproduction was by way of an RCA Photophone 'High Fidelity' System, which aimed at producing sound that was as near to the original as was possible at the time. The Regal was a large cinema built on the site of Ye Olde Castel Hotel, which was burnt down and subsequently demolished in August 1934. With the experience of the old hotel in mind, the Regal was built of steel and concrete and was as fireproof as the architect could make it.

Top: Why was it that ice cream always tasted better when we were young? This ice cream seller, believed to be Arthur Mayes, was caught on camera outside Number 18 High Street in Burwell sometime in the 1930s. These two eager children are looking forward to their special treat; what will it be? A Snofrute for a penny, or a threepenny choc bar? The scene will bring back many childhood memories of the 'Stop me and buy one' ice cream man. Remember how he placed a wafer in his mould, added a scoop of ice cream, spread it out and placed another wafer biscuit on top - then with a quick flip of his wrist out came the finished product, a perfectly shaped ice? Magic!

Today, things have moved on, in the ice cream business as in everything else, and it seems that wherever we live we cannot escape the jangling music that can be heard several times a day as the ice cream van tours our streets. Today's kids have a wider choice, however, than these children had, as these up-to-date vehicles will provide them with ice lollies and cold drinks as well as several different kinds of ice cream...which brings us back to our first question. Fifty years from now, will tomorrow's adults swear that ice cream tasted far better when they were children?

Events of the 1940s

WHAT'S ON?

In wartime Britain few families were without a wireless set. It was the most popular form of entertainment, and programmes such as ITMA, Music While You Work and Workers' Playtime provided the people with an escape from the harsh realities of bombing raids and ration books. In 1946 the BBC introduced the Light Programme, the Home Service and the Third Programme, which gave audiences a wider choice of listening.

GETTING AROUND

October 1948 saw the production of Britain's first new car designs since before the war. The Morris Minor was destined for fame as one of the most popular family cars, while the four-wheel-drive Land Rover answered the need for a British-made off-road vehicle. The country was deeply in the red, however, because of overseas debts incurred during the war. The post-war export drive that followed meant that British drivers had a long wait for their own new car.

SPORTING CHANCE

American World Heavyweight Boxing Champion Joe Louis, who first took the title back in 1937, ruled the world of boxing during the 1930s and 40s, making a name for himself as unbeatable. Time after time he successfully defended his title against all comers, finally retiring in 1948 after fighting an amazing 25 title bouts throughout his boxing career. Louis died in 1981 at the age of 67.

'Rock a Bye Baby' was being screened at the Victoria when these young people waited anxiously outside the cinema for their dates to turn up. The date of the photograph is the early 1960s; made in the USA in 1958, 'Rock a Bye Baby' starred Jerry Lewis as the devoted admirer of glamorous film star Marilyn Maxwell, who coaxes him into looking after her triplets by a secret marriage. The somewhat uninspired Paramount film, produced in Technicolor, was unremarkable

and drew little in the way of acclaim.

The Victoria, officially opened by the Mayor of Cambridge, Cllr E Jackson, in August 1931, was one of the city's favourite cinemas; how many readers remember going on their first date within these walls? The Victoria was built to seat an incredible 1,500 people and had all the modern conveniences of the day. It had central heating, a ventilating system that could completely change the air inside the building every ten to fifteen minutes, and an incredible Christie cinema organ that had every sound effect imaginable, from a jazz band to a bird whistle. 'A Yankee at King Arthur's Court' was the first film to be shown - and 'Spaceballs' and 'Predator' were the last, on 14th January 1988. The cinema was demolished a month later and was replaced by Marks and Spencer.

Wartime

In 1939 Britain's Prime Minister Neville Chamberlain had made his announcement to the waiting people of Britain that '...this country is at war with Germany.' Cambridge, along with the rest of the nation rolled up its sleeves and prepared for the inevitable. This war would be different from other wars. This time planes had the ability to fly further and carry a heavier load, and air raids were fully expected. Air raid shelters were obviously going to be needed, and shelters were built on open places across the town.

By the time war was declared an army of volunteers of both sexes had already been recruited to form an Air Raid Protection service. At first ARP personnel were unpaid volunteers but when war broke out in September 1939 they became paid staff. It was their job to patrol specified areas, making sure that no chinks of light broke the blackout restrictions, checking the safety of local residents, being alert for gas attacks, air raids and unexploded bombs. The exceptional work done by Air Raid Wardens in dealing with incendiaries, giving first aid to the injured, helping to rescue victims from their bombed-out properties, clearing away rubble, and a thousand and one other tasks became legendary; during the second world war nearly as many private citizens were killed as troops - and many of them were the gallant ARP wardens.

At the beginning of the war Sir Anthony Eden, Secretary of State for War, appealed in a radio broadcast for men between 17 and 65 to make up a new force, the Local Defence Volunteers, to guard vulnerable points from possible Nazi attack. Within a very short time the first men were putting their names down. At first the new force had to improvise; there were no weapons to spare and men had to rely on sticks, shotguns handed in by local people, and on sheer determination. Weapons and uniforms did not become available for several months.

In July the Local Defence Volunteers was renamed the Home Guard, and by the following year were a force to be reckoned with. Television programmes such as 'Dad's Army' have unfortunately associated the Home Guard with comedy, but in fact they performed much important work. The Guard posted sentries to watch for possible aircraft or parachute landings at likely spots such as disused aerodromes, golf courses on the outskirts of towns, local parks and racecourses. They manned anti-aircraft rocket guns, liaised with other units and with regular troops, set up communications and organised balloon barrages.

Other preparations were hastily made around the town. Place names and other identifying marks were obliterated to confuse the enemy about exactly where they were. Notices went up everywhere giving good advice to citizens on a number of issues. 'Keep Mum - she's not so dumb' warned people to take care what kind of information they passed on, as the person they were speaking to could be an enemy.

Older folk will remember how difficult it was to find certain items in the shops during the war; combs, soap, cosmetics, hairgrips, elastic, buttons, zips - all were virtually impossible to buy as factories that once produced these items had been turned over to war work. Stockings were in short supply, and resourceful women resorted to colouring their legs with gravy browning or with a mixture of sand and water. Beetroot juice was found to be a good substitute for lipstick.

Clothes rationing was introduced in 1941, and everyone had 66 coupons per year. Eleven coupons would buy a dress, and sixteen were needed for a coat. The number of coupons was later reduced to 40 per person. People were required to save material where they could - ladies' hemlines went up considerably, and skirts were not allowed to have lots of pleats. Some found clever ways around the regulations by using materials that were not rationed. Blackout material could be embroidered and made into blouses or skirts, and dyed sugar sacks were turned into curtains.

Above: War had been declared, and every citizen of Britain, young and old, male and female, was called upon to put his or her back into the war effort. Those who did not go into military service of one kind or another worked in factories, dug for victory, gave up their aluminium baths and saucepans, joined organisations and aided in any way they could. These boys from were not going to be left out; they might be too young to fight but while there were sandbags to be filled they were going to do their bit to protect their school building. Thousands of sandbags were used during World War II to protect the country and its beautiful civic buildings.

Top: The night of June 18th 1940 was a night of heartbreak for the residents of Vicarage Terrace. It was still early in the war, and though Cambridge was as well prepared for bombing raids as the rest of the country, the rescue services had experienced far more practice runs than the real thing. When the sirens sounded that night, families across the city rose wearily from their beds and made their way into their Anderson shelters or to the nearest public shelter. It was a couple of minutes to midnight when a brilliant glow suddenly lit up the night sky, and those still above ground knew that bombs had fallen somewhere in Cambridge. Word soon went around that a terrace of houses in Vicarage Terrace had been destroyed. In fact, ten people had died in the ruins of these homes; the youngest was Heather Maisie Pauline Dear, who was just five months old, and the oldest was William Langley, aged 45. Ironically, the pilot of the plane which dropped the bomb had been a student at Emmanuel College. Twenty-three years on, the Cherry Trees Club for senior citizens was set up on the spot - a fitting memorial to those who died in what turned out to be Cambridge's worst air raid of the war.

Main Picture: These land girls appear to have had little time to prepare for a chat with the King and Queen when they visited Burwell Fen on 19th June 1942. The sight of turbans, overalls and working gear did not ruffle the royal couple, however; they were proud of the way Britain was responding to the heavy demands of war. Women especially were literally putting their backs into the war effort, and were proving themselves to be competent in taking over many tasks that had up to that time been regarded as 'jobs for the boys'. Before 1944 the Women's Land Army paid its workers just £1.85 for a 50-hour working week, later rising to £2.85. Around 80,000, however, volunteered for the underpaid,

back-breaking work that in reality was far removed from the image of glamour it popularly enjoyed. The girls' headgear is typical of the 1940s; protecting the hair from dirt and dust with a 'turban' was the usual and quite sensible fashion of the day. Few housewives would tackle the chores unless their hair was covered by a scarf.

Inset: Encouraging the people in wartime Britain was taken very seriously by the King and Queen, whether it was touring the bomb sites of Coventry or Sheffield and chatting with those brave victims of death and destruction, or boosting the morale of the troops. This royal visit made in 1943 was to

Events of the 1940s

HOT OFF THE PRESS

At the end of World War II in 1945 the Allies had their first sight of the unspeakable horrors of the Nazi extermination camps they had only heard of until then. In January, 4,000 emaciated prisoners more dead than alive were liberated by the Russians from Auschwitz in Poland, where three million people, most of them Jews, were murdered. The following year 23 prominent Nazis faced justice at Nuremberg; 12 of them were sentenced to death for crimes against humanity.

THE WORLD AT LARGE

The desert area of Alamogordo in New Mexico was the scene of the first atomic bomb detonation on July 16, 1945. With an explosive power equal to more than 15,000 tons of TNT, the flash could be seen 180 miles away. President Truman judged that the bomb could secure victory over Japan with far less loss of US lives than a conventional invasion, and on 6th August the first of the new weapons was dropped on Hiroshima. Around 80,000 people died.

ROYAL WATCH

By the end of World War II, the 19-year-old Princess Elizabeth and her distant cousin Lieutenant Philip Mountbatten RN were already in love. The King and Queen approved of Elizabeth's choice of husband, though they realised that she was rather young and had not mixed with many other young men. The engagement announcement was postponed until the Princess had spent four months on tour in Africa. The couple's wedding on 20th November 1947 was a glittering occasion - the first royal pageantry since before the war.

Witchford RAF Station, and the men and their officers turned out in full force to welcome King George, Queen Elizabeth and their eldest daughter. Many an admiring eye would have been cast on Princess Elizabeth, who was just 21 years old at the time. She was young, very pretty, and unattached, and even a smile from the Princess would have knocked any out one of these young men. Elizabeth and her distant cousin, Lieutenant Philip Mountbatten RN, however, were already in love. The King and Queen approved of their daughter's choice of husband, though they felt that she was rather young and had met few young men in her life. Before any engagement announcement was made, Elizabeth was sent on a four month tour of Africa . Her decision remained unchanged, however, and she and Prince Philip married on 20th November 1947.

parties, fireworks displays and bonfires - a scene that was repeated everywhere across the length and breadth of Great Britain. The community in Eastfields held a huge party *(facing page),* and a piano was carried out of someone's parlour and pressed into service for the occasion. Its long surface doubled as a convenient table during the real business of the party - eating through mountains of potted meat sandwiches, cakes and jellies. Afterwards would come the singsong, with old favourites like 'Underneath the Arches', 'White Cliffs of Dover' and 'Sally', and perhaps - dare

Both pages: The war was over, and the citizens of Cambridge were tired of bombs, gas masks, the blackout and all the other privations of wartime Britain, and when peace was declared after six long years of war bunting was strung from house to house across every street and patriotic flags flapped gaily in the breeze. Along with the rest of Britain they found the energy to let their hair down and organise Victory Parades, street

we say it - a rendering of 'Knees up Mother Brown' from the more enthusiastic party animals. The residents of Perne Avenue also hung out the flags and partied the night away *(above),* and in Nelson Street the vicar cooperated and allowed the use of his church for the party *(top).* These residents showed a great deal of ingenuity, making their own party hats for the event. Was there a prize for the best one, we wonder?

Both pages: *The long war in Europe was over, and though some cautious souls decided to postpone their celebrations until victory was also declared in Japan, most of Cambridge opted to celebrate VE Day in fitting style - which, of course meant giving the kids a good time. Around the city fancy dress parties were planned, games, races and prizes were organised by fathers and uncles while in hundreds of kitchens the women donned their aprons and produced cakes, jellies and blancmanges by the dozen. Hertford Street celebrated with a fancy dress party (right), and miniature dancing girls in grass skirts, nurses, clowns, cowboys and Indians no doubt competed for a prize for the most imaginative costume. Which of them won? The residents of Kendal Way brought tables into the street for their party (above), and this splendid photograph captured the main action - eating the food generously provided from the ration books and store cupboards of mothers and other residents.*
Many were the effigies of

Adolf Hitler to be burnt on bonfires around Cambridge that evening. Revenge, it is said, is sweet - but vengeance did not belong to the people of Cambridge; Hitler had already gone ahead to meet his Maker. Renouncing his dream of a thousand-year Reich, he and Eva Braun had committed suicide together just the week before, on 30th April 1945. In the Pacific the war continued for a further four months; the Japanese surrendered on September 13th.
It was Britain's new Prime Minister, Clement Attlee, who brought the nation down from its euphoria with a resounding bump. He gave the country a serious warning that although Britain was once more at peace, there was no likelihood of prosperity for the country in the immediate future. Across the world countries were decimated by war, and there were worldwide food shortages. It would be several more years before people could stop using tinned dried eggs or shop for clothes without counting how many coupons they had.

Events of the 1940s

MELODY MAKERS

The songs of radio personalities such as Bing Crosby and Vera Lynn were whistled, sung and hummed everywhere during the 1940s. The 'forces' sweetheart' brought hope to war-torn Britain with 'When the Lights go on Again', while the popular crooner's 'White Christmas' is still played around Christmas time even today. Who can forget songs like 'People Will Say we're in Love', 'Don't Fence Me In', 'Zip-a-dee-doo-dah', and 'Riders in the Sky'?

INVENTION AND TECHNOLOGY

Inspired by quick-drying printers' ink, in 1945 Hungarian journalist Laszlo Biro developed a ballpoint pen which released viscous ink from its own reservoir as the writer moved the pen across the page. An American inventor was working on a similar idea at the same time, but it was Biro's name that stuck. A few years later Baron Bich developed a low cost version of the pen, and the 'Bic' ballpoint went on sale in France in 1953.

SCIENCE AND DISCOVERY

In 1943 Ukrainian-born biochemist Selman Abraham Waksman made a significant discovery. While studying organisms found in soil he discovered an antibiotic (a name Waksman himself coined) which was later found to be the very first effective treatment for tuberculosis. A major killer for thousands of years, even the writings of the ancient Egyptians contain stories of people suffering from tuberculosis. Waksman's development of strep-tomycin brought him the 1952 Nobel Prize for Medicine.

Both pages: At last, the day Britain and her allies had waited for had arrived: the second world war was over. Loudspeaker vans toured the streets, inviting the people of Cambridge to gather in the city centre for a special announcement to be made at noon. Long before the appointed time, people began to make their way to Market Hill. The trickle became a flood, and soon thousands of eager locals, to the accompaniment of rousing military music played from loudspeakers, were forming a vast crowd in the market place *(facing page)*. While they waited for the announcement, many attended a service of thanksgiving held in Great St Mary's. There was much to give thanks for: the long war was over at last and now things could begin to get back to normal. But for now, it was time to celebrate. The official gaiety started at 6pm that evening with a band parade, a Promenade Concert and community singing. Later came dancing, leading up to that all-important event - the King's speech at 9pm. More dancing and fireworks followed. Many communities decided to play safe and postpone the festivities until victory was declared in Japan later in the year. On VJ day, street parties were arranged across the city, and out came the flower vases, the good china and the precious tins of ham and salmon, carefully hoarded for this wonderful occasion. In York Street, the entire community held a street party for the children - though the grown-ups were not above donning their Union Jack aprons and joining in too *(above inset)*!

Events & occasions

Above: The Queen's coronation on 2nd June 1953 gave everyone a chance to declare their loyalty - and it was party time in Cambridge. Garlands and banners were hung in windows, lines of bunting stretched across every street, and the patriotic message emblazoned across the Guildhall was 'God Save the Queen'. Stallholders in the market worked overtime on decorating their stalls in honour of the great event - in fact the coronation was a red letter day in the diary of everyone in town. Not only were there the official events to look forward to, but there were the many street parties, dances and fireworks parties to enjoy. Perhaps a few people among the shoppers browsing in the market on the day of the photograph would have been able to watch the Westminster Abbey ceremony on television; it was the first time the coronation of a British monarch had ever been filmed. Many had never seen TV before - a difficult concept for us to grasp so many years on, when we are used to being surrounded by technology of all kinds. But for those who were privileged to be among those early viewers, the sight was one they will never forget.

Above right: Queen Elizabeth II was newly crowned, and now it was time to party. The Abbey Estate children's coronation party was obviously very well organised, even to having a specially-printed banner to mark the occasion. Mums and Dads were there to join in the fun and games, and this capable-looking young man wearing a Boys' Brigade uniform would appear to have been drafted in to help the day to go smoothly. Cambridge took the young and

pretty new Queen to their hearts. Unlike her father King George VI, Princess Elizabeth had begun her training for the throne early, when Edward VIII's abdication in 1936 made her the heir presumptive to the throne. She was only 14 years old when she broadcast messages of encouragement to the children of war-torn Britain, and as the war progressed she gradually took on more and more public duties. Many local people saw the coronation on television, and even viewed in black and white the occasion was a memorable one. The sight of the new Queen being anointed with oil and having the crown placed upon her head is one which few can forget.

Below: Cambridge is, as we all know, a city of cyclists - but isn't this taking things to extremes? At first glance, we might think that this young man has simply decided to change his mode of transport, but in fact he and his penny-farthing are part of the Poppy Rag Day activities back in November 1937. The student event was traditionally held on the nearest Saturday to 11th November - Armistice Day - with the intention of raising funds for

the British Legion. That particular Saturday, students dressed in weird and wonderful costumes paraded the streets of Cambridge, and ghosts, witches, clowns and pantomime horses moved among the crowds, rattling collecting boxes under the noses of all who were there to join in the fun.

The British Legion was formed by Field Marshall Haig in 1921 to present an answer to the problem faced by servicemen returning home disabled, most of them facing a future of unemployment and the prospect of living on a pittance. The Legion proved to be a powerful association whose caring force towards ex-servicemen and women extends to the present day.

Bottom: What has the photographer caught on camera here? Have these crowds turned out to see the circus coming to town? Far from it; in fact this parade of marvellously sturdy animals through the streets of Cambridge were the Percheron horses that were bred at the Chivers Farm at Histon. It was Stanley Chivers who first came across the powerful breed while serving in France during the second world war. The Chivers family had around 8,000 acres of orchards and farm land, and prize animals - pigs, horses, cattle and even poultry - were reared on the Chivers estate. When peace was declared Stanley Chivers remembered the Percherons he had seen, and shipped a number across to England to replace the shire horses they commonly used. Readers will know the Chivers family of 'Old English Marmalade' fame; they also produced jams, jellies, custard powder, canned fruit and much more. The company eventually merged with Hartleys and Cadbury-Schweppes.

If it were not for the bobby's helmet outlined in the foreground of this photograph, readers might well have imagined that they had been projected back into the 16th century. The scene, however, shows the preliminaries to a Tudor Fair which was held on Market Hill on 27th April 1938, and large crowds have turned out to watch the folk dancing and join in the fun, some of them using the fountain as a convenient vantage point. The period costumes were as close to the real thing as these ladies, aided by their trusty Singer sewing machines, could manage - though perhaps some of the footwear might not have been quite right....

St Michael's Court forms part of the background to the scene; the building was constructed during the 1930s as undergraduate accommodation for Caius College, with shops below on ground floor level. On the other side of Rose Crescent is Mathers & Son's jewellery shop (today Watches of Switzerland) and Mackintosh and Sons ironmongers - Cambridge's last hardware shop.

Events of the 1950s

WHAT'S ON?
Television hit Britain in a big way during the 1950s. Older readers will surely remember 'Double Your Money, Dixon of Dock Green and 'Dragnet' (whose characters' names were changed 'to protect the innocent'). Commercial television was introduced on 22nd September 1955, and Gibbs SR toothpaste were drawn out of the hat to become the first advert to be shown. Many believed adverts to be vulgar, however, and audiences were far less than had been hoped for.

GETTING AROUND
The year 1959 saw the development of the world's first practical air-cushion vehicle - better known to us as the hovercraft. The earliest model was only able to travel at slow speeds over very calm water and was unable to carry more than three passengers. The faster and smoother alternative to the sea ferry quickly caught on, and by the 1970s a 170-ton car-carrying hovercraft service had been introduced across the English Channel.

SPORTING CHANCE
The four-minute mile had remained the record since 1945, and had become regarded as virtually unbreakable. On 6th May 1954, however, Oxford University student Roger Bannister literally ran away with the record, accomplishing the seemingly impossible in three minutes 59.4 seconds. Bannister collapsed at the end of his last amazing lap, even temporarily losing his vision. By the end of the day, however, he had recovered sufficiently to celebrate his achievement in a London night club!

Two campuses sharing one high level of excellence

The story of the development of Cambridge Regional College is a fascinating one, giving as it does many insights into the changes in subsequent generations' perceptions of the educational needs and priorities of the region.

Today, Cambridge Regional College operates from two campuses - Kings Hedges and Newmarket Road. By contrast, just five years ago the College was spread over 11 sites, which are variously described in an accommodation survey carried out by the Estates Office at the time as 'a number of old Elliot-type huts' (New Street), 'a Victorian mansion' (Country Centre) and 'a disused garage held rent free' (Broad Street), as well as its 'purpose-built premises' (King's Hedges - Phase I); the other premises occupied by the College included a Youth Centre plus sundry school buildings owned by the County Council, and Victorian premises in York Street which were rented from St Columba's Church. It is a tribute to the College that it has successfully transformed such a disparate

Below: Students at Newmarket Road in the late 1930s.

organisation into the modern, well-equipped institution which has recently been distinguished by receiving a Grade 1 classification for resources from government inspectors - thus becoming the first large general further education college in the United Kingdom to attain this standard.

Of the many and various separate sites which have, over the years, played a part in the development of the College, one of the first to be established as a centre for further education was the Country Centre. At the time, the Centre itself recognised that its role was 'unusual if not unique', and its original aims during the 1940s may well arouse in a modern reader a degree of nostalgia for simpler times. As the headquarters for 'Homemaking Subjects' in the county, it organised classes, lectures, demonstrations and visits for housewives; the Rural Domestic Economy Programme, for instance, taught them how to bottle, can and preserve their fruit and vegetables, while classes were held on a variety of rural crafts, cookery, dressmaking and other homemaking skills of relevance to farmers' wives. Later the Centre also arranged programmes of evening

lectures on a variety of cultural subjects for men and women, and teacher training became an important aspect of the Centre's work; in-service classes were run for domestic science and needlework teachers from the local schools, and housewives whose work in class showed particular ability were encouraged to take proficiency tests with a view to becoming Further Education instructors themselves.

The Country Centre's first premises were at Shire Hall, where in 1950 it enrolled a total of 30 students. By 1968, with 2,305 students enrolled for courses and a further 3,219 attending lectures, demonstrations and special events, the accommodation at Shire Hall was becoming rather cramped, and indeed steps towards a move to larger premises had already begun the previous year with the purchase of a house at Howes Close, adjacent to the National Institute of Agricultural Botany on Huntingdon Road. Besides in-service courses, classes on offer now included cookery, winemaking, dressmaking, millinery, art, jewellery, flower arrangement, embroidery, and furnishing; this latter option was considered eminently suitable for young couples, as the husband could busy himself with the hammering while his wife did the delicate, creative work. Among the many different reasons put forward for studying at the Centre were 'to learn a craft, perfect a craft, for therapy reasons on doctor's advice, to fill the gap between school and training, prepare for marriage, make friends, provide a new interest in middle age or for the sheer enjoyment of doing things with other people' - not perhaps so very different from the reasons which prompt people to attend non-vocational courses today.

Top: Newmarket Road, the building on the right was to be temporary in 1945 and is still in use today!
Below: The Country Centre at Howes Close.

Following alterations to the house at Howes Close and the addition of purpose-built accommodation, the new Country Centre was opened on January 1st, 1972. Throughout many administrative changes, Howes Close was to remain an educational establishment for almost half a century; the site was subsequently taken over by the Cambridge College of Further Education, which was re-established in 1988 as the Cambridge Regional College, and the Country Centre was not finally vacated until the early 1990s.

During the late 50s, with the Country Centre catering admirably for the non-vocational needs of the region, steps had also been taken to meet the increasing local demand for vocational training. To cater for young workers in commerce and industry, the Further Education Centre had been founded in 1959, occupying five classrooms in a former primary school in Young Street, where it offered part-time GCE O-level courses, General Education courses intended mainly for junior Civil Servants and Post Office employees, Introductory and General Engineering courses, and Introductory and Craft courses in building. At the head of the Centre was the Warden, Mr G W Hibberd.

It was not long before the Young Street Centre outgrew the Victorian primary school premises, and four years later work to build an extension had begun. In that same year, 1963, a second Further Education Centre was launched in York Street following the acquisition of the York Street Mission Hall on a rental agreement from St Columba's Church; opened in 1885, the York Street Mission had been purchased for St Columba's in 1905 by Mrs Lewis and Mrs Gibson, 'to improve the condition of the poor by philanthropic and missionary work'.
During the mid-60s the Young Street Centre, with Mr J Moulding as Warden, concentrated on running day-release courses for young workers in the building and engineering sectors; examinations were held at the end of the course,

*Above right: Students taking part in a Construction Crafts lecture. **Right:** Peter Hurrell introduces HM The Queen to senior college staff and governors in 1993. The Duke of Edinburgh and the Lord Lieutenant of Cambridge are in the background.*

and successful students could then transfer to the Cambridgeshire College of Arts & Technology. Students at Young Street could also study either part or full-time to gain additional GCE O-level subjects. The Further Education Centre at York Street, meanwhile, offered courses for young people embarking on careers in the secretarial or commercial field; these included full-time courses either leading to the GCE O-level examinations or

providing secretarial and commercial training, and part-time courses for junior office staff and shop assistants.

From the outset, the students at York Street seem to have created a particularly lively community; a termly magazine called 'Reflector' was launched - with the very first issue devoted to creating a vivid reflection of Beatlemania in 1963 - and it became the custom for York Street students to take a market stall just before Christmas where they sold second-hand clothes, cakes, jam, Christmas decorations and suchlike items to raise cash for the student fund.

In 1974 measures to reorganise the provision of Further Education in the city resulted in the Young Street and York Street Further Education Centres being combined to form the Cambridge College of Further Education. The Principal of the new College was Mr G W Hibberd, previously Warden of the Young Street Further Education Centre; he had a teaching staff of 30, which included Mr Hibberd's wife, but the budget for support services was somewhat tight and he had to share his Typewriter Maintenance Technician with Cambridge College of Arts & Technology. Student enrolment in the first year stood at around 600. Originally there were three departments: Business and General Studies, Engineering, and Science; however, the following year Engineering merged with Science to form a single department.

July 1976 saw the retirement of G W Hibberd (and his wife), and Mr H Bashford, Head of Science, was appointed Temporary Principal, a post which he was to hold for almost three years due to the unfortunate demise of Mr D H Overton shortly after taking over the post of Principal in September 1978. Mr Bashford will doubtless be remembered by former students of the College who partook in the European camping expeditions during the summer - and who may now, reading this in their more mature years, better appreciate Mr Bashford's courage in taking responsibility year after year for the safety and good behaviour of 30 teenage students holidaying on the Continent!

A number of issues concerning the future administration of the College were raised during the late 70s. In 1976 there was a proposal from the Education Department that consideration should be given to setting up a joint governing body of the sixth form colleges, under a single Principal. Of more immediate urgency, however, were the concerns and proposals being voiced with regard to the College's accommodation. The Report of the Working Party on 16 to 19 provision in Cambridge, published in December 1977, expressed the wish 'to see the unsatisfactory York Street premises abandoned as

Above: *The Riverside Catering Complex, Newmarket Road Campus.* **Below:** *HRH Prince Edward meeting catering students at Cambridge Regional College in 1991.*

soon as possible' - a wish echoed by virtually all members of the College; staff were pressing for the whole College to be housed on one site; by September 1978 Brunswick School in Newmarket Road had been identified as a possible future site, and by February 1980 it had been agreed that the College would move into first Brunswick Infants School and then the Junior School as well.

Everybody began to look forward to leaving York Street. During this period the Academic Board had also been called upon to make decisions on a number of financial issues, of varying degrees of gravity. Thus it had supported, in September 1977, the request to purchase a video-tape recorder at a sum of £900; it had also recognised the necessity of acquiring a basic computing installation comprising one teletype and one VDU with a computer link to CCAH, in May 1978, and of purchasing for York Street a photocopier, at a cost of £990, and an additional VCR - now only £850. However, it had regrettably found itself unable to approve the expenditure of £100 on a cycle rack - apparently the College had become desperate to own one, and its hopes had been raised when the Education Department had found one, in Somersham, only to be dashed when the cost of transporting and installing was considered by the Board to be excessive.

Another issue which remained to be settled before the end of the decade was the appointment of a new Principal, and this was finally resolved when Peter Clark took up the post in May 1979. This was the third change of Principal during session 1978/79 (Mr Overton, Mr Bashford and Mr Clark), but thanks to the concerted efforts of all the staff the disruption was minimised and the delivery of courses was not affected; as it turned out, the only adverse effect was a rather unfortunate omission - there was no College prospectus for session 1979/80. Even this was not

as grave as it might have been, since the College's standing by now was such that it was able to recruit students even without the aid of a prospectus.

The College took over the Brunswick School buildings according to plan in the early 80s; Brunswick School provided the College with a site with a great deal of history attached to it, having been opened in 1937. Unfortunately hopes that this move would finally provide an escape from York Street were frustrated as the continuing growth in student numbers meant that the College was expanding to fill every available corner, so for the first few years of its existence Cambridge Regional College had to operate from a rather bewildering collection of premises. The question of accommodation, along with other issues surrounding the future of the 16-19 education provision in the Cambridge area, was to remain under discussion throughout the next decade. A Working Group had been set up with a view to reorganising post-16 education, and in 1987 they formulated long-term proposals that 'the whole of the CCFE be accommodated on a single site . . . at Long Road' (Long Road was at the time being used as a Sixth Form College) and 'the amalgamated Sixth Form College be located on the Hills Road site.' However, these proposals were subsequently rejected on the grounds that the Hills Road site had insufficient capacity to meet the areas' rising demand for Sixth Form College places. It was resolved instead that the Cambridge Regional College should be formed out of the Cambridge College of Further Education together with courses and students transferred from CCAT, and that a spacious new site at Kings Hedges should be developed for the new College.

Various theories have been advanced on the origins of the name of Kings Hedges; it may have derived from an encampment which stood here at the time of William the Conqueror, or it may refer to the fences, or deer-hedges, which were constructed to enclose the deer and game for

Below: *The Kings Hedges Campus of Cambridge Regional College.*

Above: Ann Limb, David Cleevely and Peter Dawe at the launch of the College website in 1999. Left: Receiving the Investors in People Award from left to right; Kim Norman CE, Cambs TEC and Business Link, Howard Whitesmith, Chair of Governors, Carol Rowe, Professional Development Manager and Ann Limb, Principal. Below: Students browse through the well stocked College Library.

Royal hunting parties in medieval times. The site at the end of the 19th century was described in the Cambridge Review dated February 4th 1897 as 'an old farm with earthworks of various kinds around an near it'.

Much research has been carried out on the site, and much has been written; suffice it to say here, that in January 1992 a new era in its history commenced when Trafalgar House Construction began work on the new College.

The development was planned in four phases, of which the first phase was the construction of three buildings linked by a Mall; the Library block, the Business Studies block and the Sports Hall, due for completion in 1993. The York Street building would then, the schedule said, be

vacated. Work went according to plan, watched with great eagerness by the staff and Phase I of the Kings Hedges building programme was opened by the Queen, accompanied by the Duke of Edinburgh, on Thursday 25th November 1993. This event, a tremendous landmark in the institution's development, was well-reported by the media and was described by Peter Hurrell, who had become Principal in April 1986, as 'the most important

day in the history of the College'. But there was still no escape from York Street; the College was in fact to remain there until 1997, when Phase III of the King's Hedges building programme, the Leah Manning Building, was opened.

This Phase was named after Leah Manning to commemorate her tremendous contribution to the improvement of education and welfare in the local community. Having trained at Homerton, Leah Manning was in 1908 offered a teaching post at New Street School, reputedly the worst school in Cambridge because of the extreme poverty and deprivation of the backwater in which it stood. She accepted the post and remained there for ten years, teaching pupils in classes as large as 70 or 80 and working tirelessly to improve conditions for the children, securing free milk for all and establishing an after-school play scheme. In addition to her role in a number of initiatives aimed at improving education in this country, her later career included an active involvement in politics as well as a special interest in the plight of the victims, particularly the children, who were suffering as a result of military conflict overseas. She supported the provision of day-release education and advocated sixth form colleges which were 'really comprehensive in character'; and it is eminently fitting that Kings Hedges should commemorate this remarkable woman who throughout her life strove for - in her own words - 'the best education to give all children a fair start in life.'

The completion of the Kings Hedges Campus and the substantial extensions and improvements to the Newmarket site which now forms the College's Newmarket Road Campus mean that the College now has the all the facilities it needs to accommodate its growing range of courses. 'A' level courses were transferred from CCAT from September 1988; from Autumn 1991 the College took responsibility for courses formerly run by AHEC, with the transfer of the non-advanced Business Studies courses, the first year BTEC Diploma in Science and all the evening GCE 'A' level courses formerly run by AHEC, followed by BTEC courses in Construction, Engineering and Science and the part-time daytime programme of 'A' levels, and finally by Foundation Art and supervisory courses. Today the College prospectus offers a comprehensive range of options in areas from Hair, Beauty and Fitness to Transport Technology, and from Performance and the Media to Engineering, with courses available through either part-time or full-time study and designed to meet the needs of all members of the community irrespective of age, background or gender. Of its 3,500 full-time students, over 700 are 'mature' students who have returned to education after a break. Studying at Cambridge Regional College not only leads to the qualifications needed for career development but also brings stimulation and enjoyment, greater confidence, opportunities to learn new skills, and personal satisfaction based on a sense of achievement.

Since 1 April 1993 Cambridge Regional College has been an independent body; as such it owns its own estate, employs its own staff and manages its own budget.

Under the leadership of its current Principal, Ann Limb, appointed in September 1996, the College has met every challenge and achieved notable success in all spheres. Employing a well-qualified and well-trained staff and committed to lifelong learning for all its employees, it gained the Investors in People award in May 1995 and was successfully reassessed in 1997. It is one of very few large general further education colleges in the UK to have obtained a Grade 1 for general resources, and FEFC inspectors also assessed the standard of teaching in the College as being significantly higher than the national average. The College has demonstrated beyond any doubt that a second chance education does not mean a second rate experience; and, committed to the belief that a culture of high achievement and quality is compatible with the practices of open access and equality, it is still striving to improve the quality, range and breadth of its service to the community and to raise standards of student achievement higher still. Cambridge Regional College is an institution with a

fascinating past and an exciting future. As for its present role, this was summed up by Dr Kim Howells as Parliamentary Under Secretary of State for Lifelong Learning, at a ceremony held in February 1998 to perform the official naming of the new buildings. He hailed Ann Limb as one of the country's best educationalists and observed that by offering such a comprehensive range of academic and vocational studies, Cambridge Regional College is a flagship for the further education sector which is the key to Britain's future.

Below: *European Union Education Committee visit April 1988.* **Right:** *Dr Kim Howells, MP, Ann Campbell, Ann Limb, Principal, Mr Howard Whitesmith, Chair of Governors and Mr John Beardsmoore at the Naming Ceremony in 1998.*

On the move

Events of the 1950s

HOT OFF THE PRESS

The 1950s seemed to be the heyday of spies, and in 1951 the activities of Guy Burgess and Donald Maclean caused a sensation in the country. Both had occupied prominent positions in the Foreign Office, while Burgess had also been a member of MI-6. Recruited by the Russians while at Cambridge University in the 1930s, the traitors provided the Soviets with a huge amount of valuable information. They disappeared in 1951, surfacing in Moscow five years later.

THE WORLD AT LARGE

Plans to develop the economies of member states into one common market came to fruition on 1st January 1958, when the EEC came into operation. The original members were France, Belgium, Luxembourg, The Netherlands, Italy, and West Germany. The Community became highly successful, achieving increased trade and prosperity across Western Europe while at the same time alleviating fear of war which lingered on after the end of World War II. Britain became a member in 1973.

An incredible five coaches were needed to take the large workforce of Joshua Taylor on their staff outing back in 1948, and early one morning these eager trippers gathered to have their image captured for the company's photograph album before embarking on their fun day out. Where were they bound for, we wonder? Great Yarmouth or Felixstowe, perhaps, or Clacton-on-Sea? Or were they off to sample the delights of Oxford Street, Buckingham Palace and the Thames? Sadly, we will never know.... The stately background for this photograph is Gonville and Caius College on the right, where academic life was portrayed by Dr Caius by three gates - Humility, Virtue and Honour, the last of which marked the way out for successful students. The elegant building on the left is Senate House, designed by architect James Gibbs and completed in 1730.

Above: A good range of petrol - including National and BP - was on offer at King & Harper's Garage in Milton Road back in 1925, and though cars were far thinner on the ground back then, there were also fewer garages where motorists could have them fixed. King & Harper's specialised in Morris cars and had motor accessories, oil and tyres on offer as well as fuel. The company did well and by the end of the 1960s had branches in Bridge Street, Hills Road and Thompsons Lane.
Milton Road was destined to become far busier as traffic levels built up over the next few decades. By the 1930s traffic accidents were becoming a real problem, not only in Cambridge but countrywide; between the end of World War I and 1930 the number of cars on Britain's roads increased from around 200,000 to more than a million, and between the two world wars a staggering 120,000 people were killed in traffic accidents. The Minister of Transport, Leslie Hore Belisha, was

concerned and called for new regulations. He introduced the first pedestrian crossings, and in 1934 the Road Traffic Act brought in the speed limit of 30mph in built up areas and made driving tests compulsory for new drivers.

Right: The staff of G Webb Automobile Engineers have strategically positioned their Ford Thames breakdown vehicle for this formal photograph, and stand proudly beside the tow truck to smile for the camera. What prompted the photograph, we wonder? Was it taken to mark a particular occasion, or did the boss one day suddenly say, 'I know - let's have our picture taken'? It's impossible to know, but interesting to speculate.... Webbs were offering stranded motorists an attractive day and night service at the time; the photograph dates back to 1947 - and Webbs still have a presence in the city.

Herbert Robinson's garage - today Mandela House - was a familiar sight in Regent Street/St Andrews Street when this busy scene was caught on camera in July 1961. The cycle and accessories shop, the families passing by, and the memory-evoking vehicles all add to the nostalgic atmosphere of the view. It's interesting to compare the contrasting designs of the vehicles parked outside; the somewhat austere design of the Ford Popular, typical of earlier decades, and the lighter, sleeker lines that developed in the post-war years, when colour was introduced into motor car design. The Ford Pop was an affordable little vehicle, and more than one reader will remember it with fondness as their very

first car. Do you remember the strange layout of the gears, with reverse where first gear would be on other cars? And the pull-out hand-brake placed under the dashboard? And the vacuum wipers that gave up when you put your foot down and flogged away like mad when you eased off the accelerator? Today's cars, we would all agree, are far more user-friendly - but do they have the same kind of character?

Events of the 1950s

MELODY MAKERS

Few teenage girls could resist the blatant sex-appeal of 'Elvis the Pelvis', though their parents were scandalised at the moody Presley's provocatively gyrating hips. The singer took America and Britain by storm with such hits as 'Jailhouse Rock', 'All Shook Up' and 'Blue Suede Shoes'. The rhythms of Bill Haley and his Comets, Buddy Holly, Chuck Berry, and Roy Orbison (who had a phenomenal three-octave voice) turned the 1950s into the Rock 'n' Roll years.

INVENTION AND TECHNOLOGY

Until the late 1950s you did not carry radios around with you. Radios were listened to at home, plugged into a mains socket in every average sitting room. Japan was in the forefront of electronic developments even then, and in 1957 the Japanese company Sony introduced the world's very first all-transistor radio - an item of new technology that was small enough to fit into your pocket. The major consumer product caught on fast - particularly with teenage listeners.

ROYAL WATCH

King George VI's health had been causing problems since 1948, when he developed thrombosis. In 1951 the King - always a heavy smoker - became ill again, and was eventually found to be suffering from lung cancer. His left lung was removed in September of 1951. In January 1952 he waved Princess Elizabeth and Prince Philip off on their tour of Africa; they were never to see him again. The King died on 5th February 1952.

Shopping spree

Above: This marvellous image really captures the flavour of the mid 1930s, with the price of Burton's overcoats as the real eye-catcher. Thirty-seven shillings - £1.85 in today's decimal currency - would seem to be a real bargain until we take into consideration the fact that the average weekly wage back then was not exactly what it is today!

The shop windows have just been cleaned (note the bucket and ladder used by the window cleaner), and the image of passers-by and the nearby Central Hotel is mirrored perfectly in the sparkling glass.

The lady shopper is elegant in her fur coat - a major fashion statement at the time; several more decades would pass before the tide of public opinion swung against the wearing of genuine furs. The photograph, taken from the end of Petty Cury sometime before the old Guildhall was demolished, takes in the view across Market Square. Fortunately the building housing Barrett's shop at the time survived and is today a branch of Barclays Bank, with HSBC next door; Top Man has now replaced Burtons on the right.

Right: This glimpse back in time shows us the open air market in Cambridge as it was in the 1930s, bustling with life and with a character of its very own. Set against the background of Great St Mary's and St Michael's Court, this 60-year-old view of canvas-topped market stalls is still very similar today. The delivery vehicles in the foreground were typical of the day, and the lorry conveying Jack N Baldry's Table Waters deserves a mention of its own. Which of these market stalls is selling Baldry's Lime Juice and Pepsi-Cola, we wonder? It might come as a surprise to us to realise that the 1930s too were part of the 'Pepsi generation'; Coca Cola, invented in 1886, had many rivals, but Pepsi quickly 'came alive' and established itself as the main competition. We would probably agree with the advertiser's description of the drink as 'A sparkling, bracing beverage' - but 'healthful'? Perhaps a matter of opinion?

Left: When push comes to shove.... Like competitors in the Tour de France, a tightly-bunched group of eight or nine cyclists wait impatiently alongside the bus for a lorry that is impeding their progress to let them speed away and head for home. Judging by the length of the bus queue in Sidney Street, this photograph would appear to capture Cambridge in the rush hour. There is an urgency written all over the pedestrians, the cyclists and the bus queue that tells us that this is the end of a long hard day in the office or the shop. A nice cup of tea, a hot meal, and perhaps the added attraction of an evening spent in the pub, is the thought that is uppermost in all their minds. A few last minute shoppers appear to be heading for the stores, and as the blinds are still in position over a few of the shop windows, they could well have been in luck. The photograph, which looks north towards the junction of Sidney Street with Market Street, was taken in 1950.

Above: The University Arms in the 1960s; how many readers remember the well-known hotel when it still had its glass canopy? Modernisation would eventually change the character of the frontage and leave it with the architectural style that was typical of the second half of the 20th century. Registered with the Royal Automobile Club, the 1967 RAC handbook records the fact that the University Arms Hotel in Regent Street rated four stars ('Exceptionally well appointed...a high standard of comfort and cuisine') and boasted a total of 126 bedrooms. Back then, you could enjoy a good evening meal for 17/- (85p), while if you decided to spend the night there, bed and breakfast would have set you back between £2.5s and £5.10s. - a snip, it would seem, judging by today's prices, until we take into consideration the average salary at the time.

Tulips, lilies, irises, narcissi - they were all on offer in Cambridge Market, where the containers of daffodils and tulips (or roses and chrysanthemums, according to the time of year)were the first cheerful sight that greeted the eye as you crossed to the market from the end of Peas Hill *(main picture)*. Shoppers in this 1950s view of the market square seem to be debating whether to treat their wives, or perhaps their mothers, to a cheerful bunch of flowers.
Market Hill has been the heart of Cambridge life since medieval days, when produce was sold in separate sections

of the market. Fruit and vegetables had their own part, as did milk and corn. Meat, poultry and butter was sold in the Shambles, at the southern end. The market place served as an entertainment centre as well as a place to buy and sell goods, and it was here that the sport of bull baiting had its enthusiastic followers. Baiting of a different kind took place at the pillory and the stocks, where those unfortunates sentenced to a few hours' punishment - deserved or not - would suffer the taunts - and possibly the odd bad egg or rotten fruit - thrown by those visiting the market. To them

Events of the 1960s

WHAT'S ON?

Television comedy came into its own in the 1960s, and many of the shows that were favourites then went on to become classics. 'On the Buses', 'Steptoe and Son', 'Till Death Us Do Part' and 'The Army Game' kept audiences laughing, while the incredible talents of Morecambe and Wise, the wit of Des O'Connor - often the butt of the duo's jokes - and the antics of Benny Hill established them for ever in the nation's affections.

GETTING AROUND

The 2nd March 1969 was a landmark in the history of aviation. The Anglo-French supersonic airliner Concorde took off for the first time from Toulouse in France. Concorde, which can cruise at almost twice the speed of sound, was designed to fly from London to New York in an incredible three hours twenty minutes. The event took place just weeks after the Boeing 747, which can carry 500 passengers to Concorde's modest 100, made its first flight.

SPORTING CHANCE

Wembley Stadium saw scenes of jubilation when on 30th July 1966 England beat West Germany 4-2 in the World Cup. The match, played in a mixture of sunshine and showers, had been a nailbiting experience for players and spectators alike from the very beginning when Germany scored only thirteen minutes into the game. It was Geoff Hurst's two dramatic goals scored in extra time that secured the victory and lifted the cup for England - at last.

this was all part of the day's entertainment, though perhaps the recipient didn't find the sport quite so entertaining!

The market site was L-shaped until, in the mid 19th century, fire swept through a whole block of buildings which was never rebuilt. Instead, the layout of the market was changed and a fountain erected in the centre. The centre of the market place is being used as a parking place in this wartime view of Market Hill taken in 1944 *(inset)*. In the background, 'Gone with the Wind', starring Vivien Leigh and Clark Gable, was being screened at the Victoria at the time; a stirring, romantic film that has never lost its appeal with cinema-goers.

It was a warm, sunny day when this photograph was taken in Sidney Street in 1955, with cyclists and shoppers in light summer dresses and shirt sleeves. The line of cycles propped against the kerb remind us of those gentler and more honest days when you could park your bike, go off and do your shopping, then expect to find it still there when you returned! The names above the windows of the stores may have changed, but Cambridge has always been a great place to shop. To the right of the photograph is Millers, Cambridge's music and instrument showroom. The 1950s saw the birth of the 'pop' song and were the heyday of the record player, and Millers' advert informed local people that

The 1950s saw the birth of 'pop' songs and were the heyday of the record player

they had 'standard and long playing records always in stock'. Readers may also remember that they also acted as box office for London and local theatre and concert tickets. Next door was H G Styles, confectioners, then of course the well loved Marks and Spencer.

Marks & Spencer has suffered from an unfortunate 'fuddy-duddy' image in recent years, but the quality of its clothing and the excellence of its food department has never been in doubt, and M & S remains the favourite store with thousands of shoppers, for under and outer wear and food. Marks and Spencer began life in Britain in the early years of the 20th century when Marks' Penny Bazaar opened up in the market in Leeds, West Yorkshire.

At work

No, in spite of appearances to the contrary, this is not a class in the art of building dolls' houses. A more detailed examination of the fascinating photograph reveals that the model being demonstrated by the teacher to a class of boys at Chesterton Road Senior School traces the domestic water system.

From the tank in the loft to the bath and wash basin in the bathroom go the pipes (probably copper ones, which had begun to replace the lead pipes that were part and parcel of plumbing systems into the 1950s and 60s), then down to the gas water heater and the taps above kitchen sink on the ground floor. And isn't that an illustration of filtration on the top floor of the house? A marvellous example of the model-maker's art - and one that most of these boys would have loved to take home with them (their sisters would have enjoyed it too!).

Events of the 1960s

HOT OFF THE PRESS
Barbed wire, concrete blocks and a wide no-man's-land divided East from West when a reinforced wall was built right across the city of Berlin in 1961. Many East Germans escaped to the West at the eleventh hour, taking with them only the possessions they could carry. The Berlin Wall divided the city - and hundreds of family members and friends - for 28 years until the collapse of Communist rule across Eastern Europe. Who can ever forget those scenes in 1989, when ordinary people themselves began to physically tear down the hated wall?

THE WORLD AT LARGE
'One giant leap for mankind' was taken on 20th July 1969, when Neil Armstrong made history as the first man to set foot on the moon. During the mission he and fellow-astronaut 'Buzz' Aldrin collected rock and soil samples, conducted scientific experiments - and had a lot of fun jumping around in the one-sixth gravity. Twenty-one hours and thirty-seven minutes after their landing they took off again in their lunar module 'Eagle' to rejoin Apollo II which was orbiting above them, proudly leaving the American flag on the Moon's surface.

ROYAL WATCH
Princess Margaret's announcement in 1960 that she was to wed photographer Antony Armstrong-Jones (later Lord Snowdon) brought sighs of relief from her immediate family. Just five years earlier the people of Britain had sympathised as the princess bowed to public and private pressure, ending her relationship with Peter Townsend, Prince Philip's former equerry. The Church (and the Queen, as its Head) frowned on the liaison as Townsend was divorced. Her marriage to Lord Snowdon itself ended in 1978.

Spicers Stationery Works was a major employer in Sawston in the mid 1950s - both photographs date from that period. How many of our readers will recognise the young women pictured here as themselves when they were in their 20s and 30s? If we could only speak to them they would be able to tell us all about the process that produced the packs of stationery, diaries, ledgers and kiddies' drawing books they are working over - and would remember how noisy it was to work in this vast

room filled with machinery (main picture)! It is interesting to note that the workers are 100 percent female, while the boss in his white coat is male.

Traditionally, British men have been regarded as the bread winners, going out to work every day to keep their wives and families. It was a woman's job to see to the children, shop for food every day, make the meals, clean the house, and wash and iron the family's clothes.

When Britain's men were called into military service during the World War II, women found themselves doing jobs they had never done before. The war changed the way of life for hundreds of men and women, turning generations of tradition upside down. It would take many more years, however, before women became accepted as efficient supervisors, overlookers and managers!

This page and following page: Long production lines characterised the Pye telecommunications factory in the 1950s, when the company was one of the main employers in Cambridge. Pye established a presence in the city more than 100 years ago, when they set up operations in Humberstone Road back in 1896. As their business expanded the company outgrew their premises and eventually moved to Cam Road. The decades of the 1950s and 60s were the heyday of

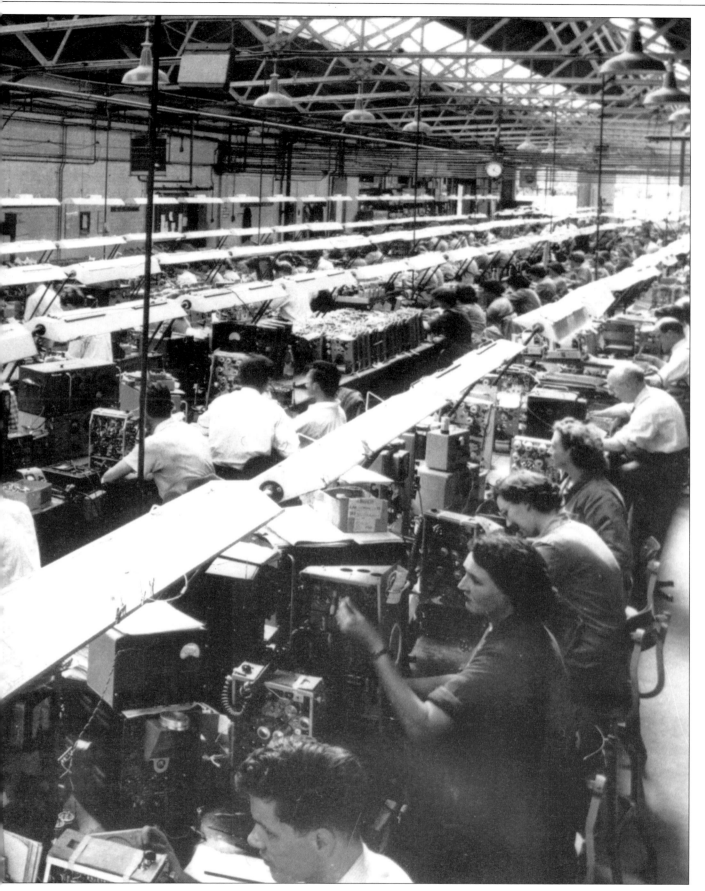

television and the transistor radio, and business was booming. Gone were the days when the 'wireless' was a large piece of equipment that stood on the sideboard in the lounge, which had to be plugged in and warmed up before the plummy tones of the BBC presenter could be heard. The transistor radio meant immediate, portable sound, and the popularity of these novel miniature radios spread like the 'flu. 'Pick a Pye for Christmas' was seen in many an advert during

the run up to the festive season, as this was the 'in' gift that Santa left under many a tree; no self-respecting teenager wanted be seen without the 'tranny' that had become the latest fashion

accessory! Pocket-sized transistor radios had been developed by the Japanese company Sony as early as 1952, though it took a few more years before companies such as Pye made them widely

Events of the 1960s

MELODY MAKERS

The 1960s: those were the days when the talented blues guitarist Jimi Hendrix shot to rock stardom, a youthful Cliff Richard charmed the nation with his 'Congratulations' and Sandie Shaw won the Eurovision Song Contest for Britain with 'Puppet on a String'. It was the combined musical talents of a group of outrageous working-class Liverpool lads, however, who formed the Beatles and took the world by storm with music that ranged from the experimental to ballads such as 'Yesterday'.

INVENTION AND TECHNOLOGY

A major step forward was made in 1960 when the laser was invented. An acronym for Light Amplification by Stimulated Emission of Radiation, the device produces a narrow beam of light that can travel for vast distances and is focused to give enormous power. Laser beams, as well as being able to carry far more information than radio waves, can also be used for surgery, cutting, drilling, welding and scores of other operations.

SCIENCE AND DISCOVERY

When the drug Thalidomide was first developed during the 1950s it was hailed as a wonder drug which would ease the distressing symptoms of pregnancy sickness. By the early 1960s the drug's terrible side effects were being discovered, when more than 3000 babies had been born with severe birth defects. Malformed limbs, defective eyes and faulty intestines were the heart-rending legacy left by Thalidomide.

available in Britain at a price that most people could afford. The company was eventually taken over by Simoco, who demolished much of the factory that had seen so much fervent activity in earlier years.

Building on traditional skills

The Cambridge building firm of Coulson has been in existence for well over a century. It was started in 1884 by 21 year old carpenter Herbert Charles Coulson, and by 1889 Herbert and his activities were occupying living and workshop accommodation and a builder's yard at 50 Burleigh Street which he rented for £35 a year, another builder's yard and buildings in Paradise Street which he rented for five guineas a year, and a stable and hayloft at the rear of 15 Burleigh which he rented from his father, William Coulson, for £2-5s-0d a year.

On the subject of William Coulson, an interesting discovery made at the company's premises in East Road during the late 1950s was an engraved, coloured certificate, admitting William Coulson to the Cambridge branch of the Operative Society of Bricklayers, a works union. The 24" by 18" certificate was dated August 1874 and signed by the Society's General Secretary, Edwin

Coulson. It is assumed that the William Coulson to whom the certificate was issued was Herbert's father, although by 1874 he would have been close to 40 years of age. Following its discovery the certificate hung for many years in the Managing Director's office as an intriguing piece of company memorabilia.

In 1889 William Lofts joined Herbert Coulson as a partner, and they set up at premises in East Road: a large mill on the ground floor equipped with the latest woodworking machinery, a joiners' shop upstairs and a timber yard opposite. Coulson & Lofts had another yard at the rear of the Red Lion public house, and they retained Herbert's Yard in Paradise Street for stabling for their horses. By 1900 the partnership was showing a healthy, if erratic, profit margin, varying between £1,007 in 1897, £4,681 in 1899 and £1,534 in 1903 (these figures include the partners' weekly wages of £1.10s.0d each). An illustrated article in The Cambridge Graphic dated 6th July 1901 reports that Coulson & Lofts 'have executed orders in various parts of the country including Ramsgate, Broadstairs, Chelmsford, Reading and many parts of London . . . On average Messrs Coulson & Lofts have in employment 260 men. Of these there are about 50 employed at the mill and workshop. There are about 30 painters and decorators employed and there is an office staff of seven clerks.' Of course the firm also carried out a great deal of work in Cambridge, including

Above: *Charles Herbert Coulson (1863-1920).*
Below: *The workshop in the early 1900s.*

specialist tradesmen including carpenters, joiners, brick-layers paper-hangers, grainers, sign writers, hot water fitters and even bell hangers. Sales figures were rising fast, reaching £19,587 before the outbreak of war. An auditor and accountant, T F Greves, was employed to keep the firm's books. The partners' wages had crept up from £1.10s.0d a week in 1890 to £25 per month in 1908, and employees' perks included Christmas boxes of cigars or cigarettes, and an outing to Great Yarmouth in the summer of 1912 where 60 of the staff enjoyed dinner at the company's expense and consumed between them some eight gallons of lemonade. A staff football club was started in 1913. But the good times were not to last. Later that year moves began to dissolve the partnership.

As of 1st January 1914 Herbert Coulson was sole proprietor, trading as Coulson & Son. Unfortunately the settlement of the partners' respective shares proved problematic; and the timing could hardly have been worse, as the effects of the first world war made money very tight. The dispute went to the High Court and dragged on for more than three years, resulting in high legal costs and a great deal of stress to both parties. The war years were in any case difficult for the firm. There were brave attempts to carry on business as usual; a venture undertaken in 1916, involving major improvements to the premises of tailors Messrs Pratt & Company in Trinity Street, attracted a certain amount of criticism vis a vis its timing, although the handsome new frontage itself found favour; a nett loss was recorded in 1917; and of course many of the company's men were away on active service. Amongst them was Mr W G James, who had joined the company in 1911 and was to serve it for over 50 years; his jottings on the firm's early history have been of great assistance in preparing this article.

some speculative development in the area around Willis Road and Harvey Goodwin Avenue.

Herbert and William acquired further cottage properties along East Road, and in 1901 they acquired the former Michael House Grange, 37 St Andrews Street for use as a combined office and decorator's showroom, remodelling the building with oak beams, lattice windows and fine wooden furnishings. Coulson & Lofts originally took these premises on a 21-year lease, at a yearly rental of £60, but when the building came up for auction by Rutters in 1908 they were able to purchase it for £2,000. It is clear from their sales literature of the time that Herbert and William were extremely proud of their premises, and with good reason; both the East Road and St Andrews Street buildings were much admired, and were in themselves excellent examples of the quality of their handiwork. At this time, other properties were acquired in French's Road which was used as an oak seasoning store, Newmarket Road a masonry yard, Bradwell's Court and Granta Place for plumbers' store and works.

In the years preceding the first world war the company was clearly thriving. Advertising itself as builders, decorators, sanitary plumbers, shop fitters and contractors, the firm employed a full complement of

Above centre: *Two early advertisements.*
Top: *A view of the East Road timber yard at the end of the 19th century.*

Herbert Charles Coulson died in 1920, and the following year the firm was incorporated as a private Limited Company, Coulson & Son Limited. W G James, who had been appointed Manager on his return from the war, became Managing Director, and the company in its new guise continued to earn a strong reputation for high quality work. Its involvement with projects such as the New Dorothy Cafe-Restaurant and Shop on Sidney Sussex corner, begun in May 1929 and completed in June 1931, brought much publicity; other major works were undertaken for Cambridge University and many of the colleges, including the Fisher Building for Queen's College and Chapel Court for St John's. The firm also played an important role in the growth of the commercial centre of Cambridge, and constructed buildings for Pye Limited and Cambridge Instrument Company Limited. Alongside major contracts such as these, it still continued to provide 'jobbing' services for smaller customers. In 1932 Negus & Sons Limited was taken over and continued to trade as an independent subsidiary.

During the second world war, the company's resources were directed principally towards defence contracts, including work at many East Anglian air fields, coastal

Above: *Coulson's restoration work on Clare College.*
Right: *37 St Andrew's Street, home of the company from 1901 to the 1960s.*

fortifications and radar stations. Afterwards, when the provision of housing became a priority, the company turned its attention to the construction of hundreds of high quality rented dwellings for numerous local authorities and housing associations. More building work was done for Cambridge University, the colleges, the commercial and public sectors and for the expanding high tech economy in Cambridge.

Sadly, 1962 brought the death of W G James, who had been managing director since the firm's incorporation in 1921. The family connection continued, however; he was succeeded by his three sons John, Thomas and Robert, and the Coulson Building Group remains a family-run firm to this day.

During the 1960s the Small Works Department developed, with specialist sections for painting, stone masonry and high class joinery and offering householders a prompt repair service covering such small but important problems as leaking roofs, broken sash cords on windows, electrical faults and burst pipes. In 1969 Harry Langdon & Company Limited was taken over, and, like Negus, continued to trade as an independent subsidiary, dealing with small contracts and jobbing. The growing need for an experienced and efficient electrical installation team led to the formation in 1968, of Hart Electrical Limited who acted as the company's regular sub-contractor, carrying out electrical works large and small for trade and private customers. More recently, with the increased emphasis on the restoration and refurbishment of some of the fine old buildings which are part of the region's architectural heritage, Coulson Insulation and Coulson Preservation were set up to cater for this demand and provide specialist services and advice on insulation, damp proofing and building preservation.

Recent reorganisation of the corporate structure has resulted in the Group being split into three: Coulson & Son Limited, Coulson Joinery Limited and Coulson Restoration Limited. Former independent subsidiaries Hart Electrical, Harry Langdon & Company and Negus & Sons Limited have all become part of Coulson & Son Limited, and this section, under the Chairmanship of Christopher James with Philip James as managing

Left: *The works party in 1956.*
Below: *Coulson & Son children's party in 1954.*

director, is further split into three sub-divisions: Construction, Small Works and Group Services. Coulson Joinery Limited, with Stephen Terrell as Chairman and John Reynolds as managing director, specialises in the manufacture and installation of purpose-made joinery and laboratory furniture. Coulson Restoration Limited includes Coulson Insulation and Coulson Preservation, and has specialist refurbishment, masonry and painting and decorating sections; its chairman is Christopher James and its managing director is Graham Watts. The Group as a whole is chaired by Christopher James, with Stephen Terrell as managing director and Philip James as a director, and its headquarters are in Cowley Road, in the purpose-built freehold property William James House.

The Coulson Building Group is fully committed to the modern approach to training and quality management, and has been able to combine its traditional strengths of specialist skills and good craftsmanship with the advantages derived from the establishment of formalised approved working practices, quality control mechanisms and apprenticeship training schemes. Having remained fully committed to retaining its workforce of skilled craftsmen through the recession, when there was little demand for specialist skills, this investment has worked to the Group's advantage in recent years.

As well as many restoration projects in Cambridge itself, Coulson Restoration has undertaken an extensive programme of vital restoration work for the railways in conjunction with the Railway Heritage Trust, beginning with the restoration of the old railway station at Bury St Edmunds in 1994. Coulson Restoration's efforts in completely transforming this previously run-down

building were recognised by the award of the inaugural national Brick Award from the Brick Development Association.

Throughout Cambridge there are examples of the consistently high quality of craftsmanship which this exceptional building company has been practising for more than a century. For the colleges, Coulson has recently been responsible for creating the spectacular new library at Jesus College Cambridge, where the company has used a wide range of specialist materials to create a fine new building with vaulted ceiling and the intricate details which harmonises completely with the famous architecture, some of it dating back 500 years, which surrounds it and for Downing College the Howard

Above: *The opening of William James House in 1988. Robert James is seen here with Baroness Blatch.*
Top: *A staff party in 1950.*

Building. The company has also built residential and student accommodation for Peterhouse, Girton College, Trinity College and Wesley House among others, while former managing director John James himself was very partial to the work which Coulson carried out on the Senior Combination Room for Downing College, feeling that the blend of modern architecture with the palladian style of the old building was particularly effective. For the University, the company has constructed an extension to the Fitzwilliam Museum and new buildings to the Faculty of Music, the Faculty of Classics and the School of Clinical Medicine at Addenbrooke's Hospital. Elsewhere in the city, the marble flooring and walls and the leather-fronted counters and the impressive gilding of Barclays Bank in Bene't Street is a result of Coulson's renovation work, and Cintra House, Trinity Hall, the Securicor building and St Peter's Swimming Pool, Huntingdon, provide diverse examples of the company's work.

Ecclesiastical work was a specialism of the firm in the early part of the century, and the renovation and repair of churches remains a significant activity today. Repair and restoration work has been undertaken on many parish churches, and when part of the medieval Ickleton Church

was destroyed by fire, Coulson rebuilt the damaged portion with stonework and timberwork to match the existing structures. Coulson Joinery has also been involved in some interesting ecclesiastical projects, including the creation of the beautiful spiral staircase in Leiston Abbey, Suffolk, which was made in the workshop to a design based on an illustration of a 'self-supporting stair', found in a 19th century joiner's handbook called 'The Stairbuilder and Handrailer'. The fine craftsmanship of Coulson Joinery can also be seen in offices and reception areas throughout the city, while at Island Hall, Godmanchester, the exquisite Chinese Bridge was designed to match the style and elegance of the original 1750s bridge and constructed entirely out of English Oak.

Herbert Coulson entered the 20th century as an enterprising, highly-skilled carpenter who took great pride in his work, set himself rigorous standards and enjoyed an excellent reputation for quality built up over a couple of decades. The Coulson Building Group will enter the 21st century as a forward-looking, family-run company with a highly-skilled workforce which takes great pride in its work, sets itself rigorous standards and enjoys an excellent reputation for quality built up over more than a century. In the intervening years, Coulson, as the leading independent building company in Mid-Anglia, has contributed a great deal to the development of Cambridge and the surrounding area, both in the form of new buildings and in the safeguarding of the region's cherished heritage through its expert restoration and preservation work. We trust that the Group's well-deserved success will continue through the 21st century and beyond.

Left: The Headquarters of Coulson Building Group today. Below: The current board - from left to right: Stephen Terrell, Philip James and Christopher James.

Red and bursting with Energy

There is something typically British about the colour red. It is a shade we associate with some of our most prized traditions. Where would we be without the jolly red post box or the double decker bus? Whoever it was who tried to do away with our phone boxes had it wrong, because the old style, painted in the proper colour, is on its way back. Seeing the red van of the postman trundling long the country lanes is a glad sight for those of us waiting for a message from a relative or loved one. The same thought must have inspired Shelford Energy, or Shelford Petroleum Oil Transport Company, as it once was known. The distinctive red of their tankers and vans have become a common sight in and around the village of Great Shelford for some 35 years. Keeping the home fires burning, and those of industry too, has been entrusted to the company since around 1963. It was in the mid 90s that the name 'Shelford Energy' was born. The focus had been on distributing heating oils to homes and businesses in the area, backed by a service offering the maintenance of oil burner equipment. As the end of

the millennium approached, a new direction was thought to be best in meeting the needs of a new age. It wanted to let its customers know that, as well as its business activities, there was a greater variety and range of products on offer. The change of name presented a more focused approach to a business that was more than just the distribution of heating oil for agricultural, industrial and domestic use. Shelford Energy was now offering a full service by providing boiler installation and an all year round repair service. All this has been backed by a set of sales and field personnel who have been trained and selected to deliver a fast and efficient service.

The tankers may have only been moving around Cambridge for less than four decades, but the connection with keeping people warm and the wheels of industry turning go way back to the 19th century. Richard Headley owned some land in High Green which he

Telegrams: Corn Company, Shelford, Cambs.

THE
Shelford Corn & Coal Co.,
GREAT SHELFORD, Cambs.

COAL, CORN, SEED, CAKE, SALT & MANURE MERCHANTS.

Miller's Offal, Malt Dust, Hay, Straw, Chaff, Moss Litter, &c.

LOWEST MARKET PRICES FOR CASH.

Above: *One of the company's early business cards.*
Below: *An early Morris lorry used for house-to-house coal deliveries.*

opposite journey and so it was that Great Shelford's connection with the coal supply industry was begun. By 1906 the yard and coal store had come to be known as the Shelford Corn and Coal Company. It was then owned by Messrs Wright and Kent who had taken on a certain Mr Clarence Edwin George after he left school at the turn of the century. It was to be the George family that would take the company through the greater part of the 20th century as it prospered and grew. It may seem strange to link coal with corn, but there was a great deal of arable farming of cereal crops close to the village. In the 1920s there were still four other corn merchants in Great Shelford alone. The company kept its own horses stabled on site and, early in the morning, it was a common sight to see them being harnessed to carts ready to take coal around the neighbouring hamlets. In 1905, you had your choice of Wallsend cobbles, Staveley kibbles and Smithy nuts. Briquettes came at 1s 8d for a cwt. Ask anyone under 30 what that means, much less to work out the price per ton, and you will get a funny look. Mr Clarence George took over the reins as the managing director in the mid-1930s,

exchanged for 11 acres at the corner of London Road and Station Road. The days of the railways were just dawning and, in 1845, the London to Cambridge Railway was built. As the lines passed across his land, Richard saw his opportunity. Having access to the railway sidings, he built the Railway Tavern and a yard, malting and coal store. His idea was to be involved in the two way movement of goods. The malt would go to the breweries in London and coal would make the

following the retirement of the owners. He rose to become chairman of the company by the late 1940s and by this time, the George family owned 98 per cent of the company shares. Clarence worked right up to his death in 1967, aged 78. The family decided to release its

*Above: The original premises between the maltings and the station pub with the drying kiln shown in the far right background. **Below:** The next step...*

THE SHELFORD CORN & COAL CO. LTD.

shares in 1980, but kept nearly half of the property where Shelford Petroleum operated. After the closure of the Corn and Coal Company, in 1986 the George's bought back the part of the property they had released. They had already shown their own interest in land by buying a farm to the west of the city in 1956. Originally 245 acres, it had grown to over 600 acres by the time it was sold in 1989.

Great strides were made between 1940 and the early 1960s. A tall grain silo and dryer were built and malting barley was transported in bulk directly onto the railway wagons in the siding that Richard Headley had spied 100 years before. Talk of forward planning! Burtons Ales and other breweries along the Trent were thankful for his

foresight. Realising that local companies were turning to oil for their fuel needs, the Shelford Corn and Coal Company started to supply them in a small way in the 1950s. Spotting the way forward, the George family established a separate company in 1963 which initially sold paraffin oils and went on to supply the central heating oils we are familiar with today. The Shelford Petroleum Oil Transport Company had arrived. It had no connection with any of the major oil companies, though Regent Oil (later Texaco) offered the Corn and Coal Company a chance to distribute its products in the area. Always very much a family firm, with a well developed portfolio of clients, the George family wanted to retain control over its own future and so bought oil on the open market. The future looked to be one of oil

fired central heating in the home. It was plentiful and relatively cheap. The established coal customers, both commercial and domestic, would stay with the firm and it would be natural for them to stay with a company they knew and trusted. The corn business also meant that Shelford Petroleum was well connected with agriculture. For years farmers had dealt with the George family when corn was being transported as well as coal supplies and so it was only common sense for them to come to Shelford Petroleum for their fuel requirements as well. For the first 10 years or so business boomed. However, by the end of the 1970s, a different picture

Above: *A Shelford tanker at Audley End.*
Top: *The first paraffin delivery tanker.*

was drawn. High inflation, the world recession, huge price rises by the OPEC countries and a corresponding fall in price, in real terms, of gas and coke meant difficult times for the industry. In the years that the company has been in existence, prices have increased by over 1,000 per cent. However, over the last few years the economy seems to have bottomed out and be on the way back up again and Shelford Energy is looking forward to the times ahead with great enthusiasm and optimism. All the time the family firm has tried to provide an efficient local service to a set of loyal customers who have needs that the national major companies cannot serve. They lack the flexibility and the personal touch. Shelford Energy knows the locality and the community intimately. It can draw on over a century of trade, in one form or another. Committed to its locality, it has a policy of reinvesting its profits for future development and in contributing to community life and taking responsibility for the environment. That

is not just pious thinking. In the drought of 1976, the company was involved in Operation Rodeo. Fuel was delivered every day to keep the water pumps going on the River Ouse during its emergency diversion. Storage tanks were sited and plans made to pump 20 million gallons of water a day for 100 days at Grafham Water. Shelford Energy can look forward to a future as the place to come for all your heating needs, knowing that it is built on a successful and caring foundation.

Above: *A modern Shelford Energy tanker with environmentally friendly design features.* ***Left:*** *An articulated tanker alongside the very first Concord exhibit at the Imperial War Museum in Duxford.* ***Below:*** *The tanker fleet in the early 1980s.*

Building material success out of traditional family values

Today Ridgeons has more than 650 employees, 90 lorries, numerous branches in and around Cambridge, and stocks just about everything a builder could ever need; and all this has grown out of the enterprise of one man and a bicycle, dealing with one product - wood.

The founder of the company was Cyril Ridgeon, the grandfather of the current Chairman. In 1911 he converted one of the bedrooms in his house in St Barnabas Road into an office and began working as a merchant for timber importer Bristow & Copley who imported softwood into the port of Kings Lynn. From there Cyril's stocks were transported to Cambridge by rail. He worked on his own for a year, and by then the business was sufficiently well established for him to take on an assistant; Mr W J Cornell looked after things in Cambridge while Cyril travelled around, by train and pushbike, visiting potential customers. The following year the business was doing so well a little hut was built in the railway sidings at Tenison Road, where his deliveries arrived, and nephew Leslie

Ridgeon joined the firm; but when war broke out in 1914 Cyril's entire workforce of two was called up.

In 1918 they both returned to find that Cyril had spent the war doing useful things like organising the village carpenters into making ammunition boxes for the Ministry, which had kept the firm going. The business now began to expand. Deliveries were made by hand cart or by horse and cart, with Dave Langley employed to drive the horse; more and more men were employed, including Cyril's brother Horace who became yard foreman and William Cullum who drove the first lorry, an ex-army Wolverine purchased in 1923. Subsequent additions to the motorised fleet included a solid-tyred Daimler 3-ton lorry, a Leyland 5-ton lorry, a 30 cwt Ford lorry, two 30 cwt Chevrolet trucks, and two tractor units, a Fordson and an International, with draw-bar trailers. This represented some considerable investment, made possible by high turnover which was a result of the tremendous activity in the building industry during that period. A great quantity of new housing was being put up by local builders, and the town centre was undergoing much redevelopment as well, while the growth in the market for bathroom fittings provided another useful sideline for Ridgeon - having a bathroom in a house was a new idea which really caught on during the 1930s. New materials were being developed, too,

Above left: *Cyril Ridgeon, founder of the company.*
Below: *Ridgeon's premises in the 1930s.*

such as 'Essex board' (a laminated paper board), Asbestos and, later, plasterboard, all of which Ridgeon stocked. By 1931 brother Robert was running a second timber storage site on Cavendish Road; some £2,000 was invested in installing a sawmill driven by a Ruston Hornsby engine; and the following year the company was registered as a limited company.

One of Ridgeons' first actions as a limited company was to start a private pension scheme, making it one of the first firms to do so. Cyril had always believed in looking after his workers. Not only did his employees get a week's paid holidays, which was quite unusual for manual and shop-floor workers at this time, but they also enjoyed regular staff outings; the precedent had been set with a trip to the Empire Exhibition at Wembley in 1925, mainly because the

Above: An early staff outing.
Top: A staff outing in June 1953.
Right: Elliot Ridgeon, managing director from 1942 to 1973.

company had supplied building materials for the Exhibition, and during the 1930s coach trips for staff and their wives became an annual event, with trips to Clacton in 1930, Great Yarmouth in 1931, Southend in 1932 and Felixstowe in 1933. In 1934 Ridgeons, Rattee & Kent and Heffers Printing Works organised a combined staff outing to Brighton, travelling on a special train which left Cambridge before 6 am on the Saturday morning!

Appreciation of the workforce's contribution has always been an important principle at Ridgeons; staff were trained to serve the customers promptly, efficiently and courteously, and in the 1930s the work was physically demanding as well. At the Cavendish Road premises, which were originally used simply as a warehouse, all timber was stacked by hand after being unloaded from the railway trucks. Later Cavendish Road also became a fireplace manufacturing site when independent slab tiled fireplace surrounds became popular, and in 1935 new showrooms were opened in Hobson Street where fireplaces and Aga cookers were displayed.

Cyril's son Elliot Ridgeon became Managing Director in 1942 after his father's death, and, like his father,

Elliot found himself having to adapt to wartime conditions when he had only been running the business for a few years. The second world war brought the firm's expansion to an abrupt halt. As in the first war, Ridgeons contributed to the war effort, but this time it was better placed to play a significant role, and it became a strategic depot for the storage of timber on behalf of the Government. A system was developed whereby strategic stocks of timber and plywood, and sometimes tarpaulins and other items, were stored at various locations so that if one site were to be hit, the entire stock would not be destroyed. A network was built up with 'satellite' depots at various Cambridgeshire villages such as Toft, Harston and Linton, and when timber or other material was 'called off' for emergency repairs in London, it would either be collected by the Army, or one of Ridgeon's drivers would take the order down on one of the firm's lorries, usually overnight and often after a day's work.

Eventually peace returned and Ridgeons began to concentrate once again on stocking up with a full range of building materials to meet the needs of the construction industry, and the last 50 years have seen the gradual evolution of the company into the Ridgeons of today. This has taken the form of continuous development, improvement and expansion, but the principles upon which the firm was founded - customer care, staff loyalty and family commitment - have remained the same.

Ridgeons has been the market leaders for the supply of all building materials in Cambridge for many years, stocking some 50,000 lines and also offering such specialist services as computerised paint mixing and precision timber machining to minute tolerances, a service of especial value to the picture frame industry. A carefully-planned network of branches at strategic locations throughout East Anglia (reminiscent, perhaps, of the company's logistical exercises in the second world war, but on a larger scale) brings the Ridgeons range of products within reach of as many builders, plumbers, heating engineers, main contractors and members of the general public as possible. In Cambridge, meanwhile, Ridgeons concluded, after extensive market research, that the best way to serve its customers would be by having two outlets, one to the north and one to the south; the Cambridge North branch in Nuffield Road duly opened in 1995 and a year later, following a total redesign and refurbishment, the old Cavendish Road site reopened as the Cambridge South branch, now accessed via

Above left: *David CE Ridgeon, the present chairman.*
Below: *The Cromwell Road site was officially opened in July 1997 by HRH The Duke of Edinburgh.*

Cromwell Road. The firm moved out of Tenison Road in 1996, having spent 85 years there, but has not completely severed its connection with its original home as its Octopus Home Centre, opened in 1980, now occupies part of the site.

The smooth running of the company's extensive operations depends upon a loyal staff of around 650, of whom almost a third have been with the firm for more than 10 years; regular presentations of long-service awards are made on completion of 10, 15 or 20 years' service. Ridgeons' commitment to staff development and training has earned it the prestigious Investors in People quality standard. In an environment where continued success depends on the introduction of new technology and modern working practices, the firm has been careful to manage change in a way which suits the staff and preserves the all-important friendly, family atmosphere. Since the workforce is now too large to be taken on a single annual coach trip, the Community & Social committee organises all kinds of trips - to stately homes, the seaside, amusement parks with 'white knuckle rides' or by shuttle across to Boulogne - as well as many other social events, from inter-branch football matches, bowling and quiz nights to pantomime; and everyone is kept in touch with all the goings-on through the bi-monthly newsletter, The Ridgeon Recorder. Fundraising events are held regularly to support various charities and the management is also generous in its donations. One very important club is the '25 Club', a register of full or part-time staff with over 25 years' service; at the time of writing the club has 194 past and present members, one of whom is the current Chairman, David C E Ridgeon, who joined in January 1953.

David and his brother Michael represent the third generation of the founding family, being Elliot's sons and Cyril's grandsons, and the family connection is already assured for the next generation through the involvement of David's daughter, Anne and Michael's son, Gordon. The family philosophy of caring for the customer, which has characterised this company from the start and which is more in evidence than ever today, will therefore be carried forward into the next century.

Above left: *The Cromwell Road site today.*
Top: *One of the six Long Service awards in April 1999.*

Cecil Instruments: high-tech and flying high

Cambridge has its own version of Silicon Valley in the Milton Technical Centre. It is here that you will find Cecil Instruments Ltd, the brainchild of physicist, Cecil Tarbet. High-tech in Cambridge seems a far cry from the dons and chairs of learning and teaching that everyone thinks of when the city is mentioned. But, the computer chip age is firmly established here. The world of spectrophotometry and liquid chromatography has arrived. Long before Bill Gates had been heard of, Cecil Tarbet was ploughing his distinctive

furrow across the world of optics, wavelengths and spectral curves. Like many a new business, it grew from humble beginnings. How often is it that British innovation and verve have had to develop from a back room, outhouse or tiny lock up? Cecil Instruments was no different. In its case, the environment was Mr Tarbet's own garage and the studio wing of his house. In 1968, when he took the plunge, the workforce was limited to just three women. None of them had any training in the field of electronics. It was very much a matter of learning on the job. To keep things 'in the family', one of these good souls had been the Tarbet nanny! Having helped in the bringing up of Cecil's daughter, she was now to help nurse a new child into its technical adolescence. Fortunately, she brought some knowledge of spectrophotometry with her, having worked in a haematology department. So, it was not all gobbledy gook to everyone. She later married and left the company, but one of the original 'Holy

Left: *Mr Cecil Tarbet obtained the very first I.D.C. It was used to open the Science Park in Cambridge. He later decided to develop his own site in Milton.* **Below:** *Company headquarters in Milton.*

Above and left: *Scientists analysing biological samples in Cecil Instruments' laboratories.*

days, the total number employed has remained steady at around 50 or so for several years. This has helped keep the intimate feel and the sense of pulling together. It is hardly surprising that a number of employees have been with the company for over 20 years, a sure sign of job satisfaction.

The world of pre-programmed spectrophotometers, tablet dissolution, reflectance and chromatography requires a high degree of expertise. Cecil Tarbet gained much of that in his time at Unicam. There he had risen to head the design and development department, with a force of 100 team members answering to him. Additionally, he had become a company director. However, anxieties were common in the firm as the Dutch giant, Philips, was preparing a take-over bid. Mr Tarbet decided to go it alone, though not without a gulp or two when considering what he might be

Trinity' is still on the payroll. Over 30 years on she can be found supervising instrument assembly. This feeling of togetherness is important in promoting good relationships and keeping up staff morale. This is noticeable at Cecil Instruments. Although the business has expanded dramatically since those early

letting himself in for. Even he was tempted when the deputy chairman of the Pye Group head-hunted him two years later and offered him the role of managing director of Pye Unicam. But, his determination to be a master of his own destiny meant that this independent spirit remained free. Even Charles Harmer, who had made the offer, agreed that Cecil was right to refuse the opportunity when they met some years later. It took Mr Tarbet a week to decide, so attractive was the opening, but it was a decision he never came to regret.

If not regrets, he was to suffer frustration in his first attempts to grow from the cottage industry of his own home. Although he had success, the business had to expand or risk being not much more than a paid hobby. It had gone well. The first product, an automatic colourimeter, was sold from a small stand taken at the Labex exhibition in the capital. The first sale was the longest imaginable, being to Australia. There was almost something preordained about this. Exports now form 80 per cent of the business. Orders poured in for the technically revolutionary new instruments and, in order to cope, rented buildings were taken on Trinity Hall Farm Industrial Estate, south of St John's Innovation Centre. Further expansion into a former farmhouse, the installation of two mobile homes and offices and

> *"Long before Bill Gates had been heard of, Cecil Tarbet was ploughing his distinctive furrow across the world of cells, wavelengths and quadratic curves."*

a showroom on Chesterton Road followed. Then came the frustration. By now, Mr Tarbet was spending (and wasting) considerable time in travelling from one site to another. In 1970, he was in the car, visiting one of the company's eight buildings, when he decided to approach both Cambridge City Council and the Board of Trade for assistance. It seemed simple. Help with financial support, planning permission, development grants etc would help both the image of Cambridge, and the prosperity of the city and the nation, to boot. After all, had not the Labour Government created a Ministry of Technology and fronted it with one of its high fliers, Tony Benn? The response from the Council was cool. Cambridge was a city of culture and education. Industry meant smelly chimneys and grime. It was far more suited to Tyneside or Merseyside, where the dole queues would be glad to see factories being built. The nearest that these Council members had come to high-tech was the ability to accept that colour TV was here to stay! The Board of Trade had similar dinosaur views. An old fashioned set of values and concepts was strangling Cecil Instruments at birth. Just as he was about to

Below: *Part of the Instrument Assembly department in early 1976.*

Above: *The Applications and Training Centre.*

bang his head against another brick wall of bureaucracy, out of the blue came a phone call from someone within Tony Benn's Ministry. At last word had got through that here was a young and vibrant company. All that was needed was some help in kick starting the next phase of development for the only British owned company in this field. Facing a tricky meeting with the Board of Trade, Cecil Tarbet had not been optimistic that the necessary industrial development certificate would be granted. Without it, no building could take place. But, Mr Benn's department intervened and the IDC was awarded to the company. It was the very first such award of its kind; something of which Mr Tarbet is rightly proud. This IDC was used to open the Cambridge Science Park.

Everything took time to come together. It was not until 1974 that the company's various departments were housed under one roof. Now known as the Milton Technical Centre, established on the northern fringe of Cambridge, for many years half of its business was conducted with universities and colleges restocking their bio-chemistry departments. However, although there is a significant link with the higher education sector, industry has become more and more important as a focus of the company's sales. Food processing, brewing, drugs companies and the petrochemicals industry all use

Cecil Instruments in their respective fields. It does not stand still, as competition is fierce, particularly from the Far East and the USA. At the Technical Centre, there is a training and research suite. Some of the more mundane work and standard components are subcontracted to other suppliers abroad and in the United Kingdom, so as to keep the more challenging work in Cambridge to stretch and motivate the work force. Sometimes, you can be too good for your own good. One of the perils of success in commerce is in attracting the attentions of the 'big boys'. Mr Tarbet feels that he should change his name by deed poll from Tarbet to Target, so often has he had to rebuff those anxious to buy him out. However, he has no plans to join the league of predators. The buying up of other small fry, to boost his image or his ego, is not for Cecil. He always has been more interested in the personal challenges that lie ahead. In his case this has included gaining his own pilot's licence. In order to visit European suppliers and customers, he bought a small fleet of private planes in the early 70s. This developed into Cecil Aviation and his planes often fly politicians and leading industrialists from the base at Marshalls. By 1977, he had gained his own 'wings'. When asked, 'Why?' he replied, 'It was a challenge and something interesting to do.' He will keep on meeting those challenges, whether in Cambridge or somewhere else that needs him. Whatever else, if he is in his plane, you can be sure that Cecil Instruments Ltd is flying high along with him.

The company that never tyred of improving its service

It is sometimes said that the single invention which had the greatest impact on mankind's development is the wheel; and that being the case, the importance of the tyre should not be underestimated. Tyre Service Company cannot claim to have invented the tyre, but it was certainly among the very early tyre companies. It was set up in 1929 by Ernest Brown, in a small shop in Jesus Lane, where many of his customers were local cyclists. Bicycle tyres continued to account for the larger part of the firm's trade throughout the 20s and 30s, but as motor cars became a more and more common sight on Cambridge's roads, so motorists and local commercial vehicle users became more and more frequent visitors to Tyre Service Company at 11 Jesus Lane.

With an increasing variety in both makes and models of vehicles on the market, it became necessary to stock an ever-increasing range of tyres, and the time came when the shop in Jesus Lane was no longer adequate. In the early 1940s the company moved to a former mens outfitters shop at 28-30 Burleigh Street. Here Ernest could keep a larger stock and range of tyres, which were fitted to vehicles that had to be jacked-up at the kerbside. The pace of life as Ernest recalled was much more leisurely in those days; motorists were perfectly happy to watch him and his assistants working on their car at the roadside, and to stop and join him for the occasional tea-break. Ernest also used to recount tales of the war years when tyres for civilian use were in very short supply; in order to obtain stock for his customers he used to go to London, taking with him country produce and engage in a spot of bartering: eggs and vegetables helped obtain tyres and tubes.

The post-war years saw a change in peoples' lifestyle. The young had more money; living standards and expectations were rising; car ownership became a symbol of success, to which more and more families aspired. There was also a significant increase in the amount of goods

Right: *Ernest Brown, founder of the company.* **Below:** *28-30 Burleigh Street in 1950.*

being transported by road, with existing road haulage companies expanding their operations and a number of new transport companies starting up around the area. By the time Ernest's son Colin joined his father in the business in 1962, turnover had increased tremendously, and Burleigh Street was becoming too congested for comfort.

On March 1st, 1965, Tyre Service Company moved to a former grocery/butcher's premises in Histon Road. This site was sufficiently spacious for Ernest and Colin to create an accessory shop, two car bays and a fitting area, in addition to storage room for stock. Meanwhile public concerns over various aspects of road safety, including the roadworthiness of some of the vehicles on the roads, had been growing, and when Barbara Castle brought in the first tyre law specifying the minimum

By kind permission of the Cambridge Collection

Above: *182-184 Histon Road in 1965.*

level of tread depth which a tyre must have, sales at Tyre Service Company - now nicely installed in its new premises - rocketed.

Greatly increased public awareness in the importance of tyres in terms of both safety and performance led to many changes in the industry. More tyre outlets opened, taking advantage of the growing market; competition within the industry became more intense; and the customer - whether retail, trade, fleet operator or farmer - became much more demanding and discerning. In 1972 the Company was able to buy and redevelop adjoining properties, which allowed them to extend their facilities tremendously; the result was 14 easy-access car fitting bays, two commercial bays, four exhaust ramps and an ample forecourt besides offering a mobile fitting service.

The next decade was to some extent a time of adjustment within the tyre distribution industry. During the boom period it had attracted many more firms of varying degrees of professionalism. At the lower end of the scale were the cut-price, down-market tyre merchants who offered sub-standard products to those prepared to make false economies, even though by doing so they put at risk their safety and that of other road users. However, many reputable firms had also grown up, supplied by the major tyre

manufacturers who had dramatically increased production and at the same time improved tyre quality, and the life-expectancy of their products significantly. All this resulted in massive over-production and over-marketing. Tyre Service Company's policy of continually updating and improving the services it offered meant that its position at the forefront of the industry would help to secure its future; with radio-controlled vehicles, a 24-hour service and a high calibre of staff to handle the sophisticated equipment which had been installed both on the workshop floor and in the office, the level of customer care was second to none. However, as a family firm in competition with multi-national, multi-depot conglomerates, diversification seemed a wise policy; so in 1981 Tyre Service Company took over Cambridge Battery Service, whose founder Jim Truelove had just retired. Jim had started and developed the business, rebuilding and supplying batteries for all manner of vehicles from cars and motorcycles to tractors, diggers, crawlers, combines, commercial vehicles and even Outside Broadcasting Units, and, in the days before batteries became sealed units, offering a repair service. In fact it was one of the last firms to offer this service, and motorists, farmers and fleet operators from miles around used to bring their old-style batteries to Cambridge Battery Service for repair or replacement.

On becoming Managing Director of Cambridge Battery Service, Colin Brown made various improvements, extending the premises, building a new car park and introducing new technology such as the latest electronic wheel alignment system. The services available to customers from this very diverse local company included engine tuning, brake and exhaust replacement, M.O.T. testing, diesel pump and injector servicing, car automotive parts, power tools, electric motor rewinding, all auto-electrical repair work including the sales and fitting of in-car entertainment systems, one of the first companies locally to sell mobile telephones and of course the sale and repair of batteries.

By the end of the 1980s the Histon Tyre Service Group of Companies had been formed; besides Cambridge Battery Service Limited and the original tyre business in Histon Road, (renamed Cambridge Tyre Service Limited in 1986) the Group consisted of depots in Haverhill, Newmarket

Below: 162-180 Histon Road in 1985.

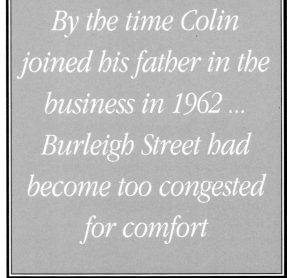

By the time Colin joined his father in the business in 1962 ... Burleigh Street had become too congested for comfort

and Bar Hill, P. H. Allin Motorcyles acquired in 1981 and a new taxi meter manufacturing unit, Cambridge Development and Communications. No doubt some readers will remember buying their first motorcycle from P. H. Allin; this company was in fact the first motorcycle dealership in Cambridge, which at one time held the franchise for the famous Scott marque and was subsequently the main Yamaha dealer later acquiring the Honda and Triumph main agencies making them the leading motorcycle dealer in the area.

Over the years the Histon Tyre Service Group tried hard to offer a high level of service and customer care in all its subsidiaries besides remaining competitive, endeavouring to do its best by offering a choice of top quality goods and over the years the Company played its part in educating the motoring public in ways in which they can take to avoid putting themselves at risk. For instance, when the refurbished Cambridge Battery Service premises were opened in 1981 a two-day Electrical Automotive Safety Show was mounted in conjunction with the police; one thought-provoking element of the show was a Black Museum which included various horrifying items collected by the police at the scene of road accidents in Cambridge, and

featured brake shoes worn down to the metal and a burnt-out electrical harness from a car where the motorist had used a one-inch nail to replace a blown fuse!

On a lighter note, readers may remember that Cambridge Tyre Service sponsored the Cambridgeshire Premier Football League in the 1980s and continued to support other local events generously. The success of the company has also provided employment for a considerable number of local people, and their employees enjoyed excellent training and career prospects, alongside all the traditional benefits of working for a family-run business with a first class reputation. However, the Management became increasingly concerned about the concentration of their competition being in the hands of fewer but much larger companies so when the opportunity came to sell their Newmarket Road premises and its various specialist divisions in 1989 it reluctantly closed a fasci-

nating chapter on a well known local landmark. This was followed in 1991 by an approach to integrate their tyre business with a much larger company.

By then the market had become increasingly difficult for the smaller independent tyre distributor to compete in so the directors decided to sell and help secure the future of its loyal and in many cases long serving staff and it is now part of a multi-national organisation. The taxi-meter manufacturing business was subject to a management buy-out and moved to other premises. The story was then completed when after the rapid expansion of the motorcycle market, P.H. Allin was approached by a public company anxious to expand its interest in this business and was subsequently sold in 1997.

The original holding company, Histon Tyre Service Limited, is still run by Colin Brown, and remains committed to the belief that whatever new developments the company engage in during the next millennium, how customers are treated and the service provided to them remain the most important things of all.

Top: Allin's motorcycle premises before redevelopment. Right: Colin Brown. Below: 182-184 Histon Road in 1990.

For the benefit of Cambridgemen

On 19th January 1850, at a meeting with the Mayor of Cambridge held at the Town Hall it was agreed to set up a society to be known as the 'Cambridgeshire Permanent Benefit Building Society'. The object of the building society was to 'make every man his own landlord'. The new building society was quite independent of politics and open to all. Meetings were held monthly at Charles Wisbey's Auction Room, Trinity Street, Cambridge.

So successful was the society that local people regarded it as an organ for investment superior to any other schemes then available to people of modest incomes. Before the development of the building society movement these had been unable to invest their savings other than in privately run local banks, often a risky business. Canal and railway companies, like other industries, set minimum stakes well above the funds held by small tenants and others of limited means. One of the success stories among Cambridge Building Society members is that of the Victorian bricklayer who used his loan to buy land on which he built two houses. He rented out the second house to pay off the loan while he lived rent free, as a modest capitalist, in the first. It is from such beginnings that many a thriving local, even national, business has grown.

During the first years the society needed to borrow from the banks to meet the demand for mortgages. By 1875 there were 3,362 shares in existence and £109,353 outstanding on mortgages.

Local Offices were established at St Neots, St Ives and agents were set up at Soham and Biggleswade. The last of the original branch offices to survive was at St Neots, this effectively closed on the retirement of Miss Sibley in 1946. Mr Sibley and his daughter gave 78 years loyal service to the Society and the members at St Neots.

In 1861 the society's head office moved to its first permanent home in Post Office Terrace, in a room hired from the Penny Savings Bank. As time went by the lease for this came up for sale and was purchased, at auction,

Above: *Cyril Puddick joined the society in 1936 as a clerk rising to assistant secretary in 1951 and chief executive in 1971. He retired in 1978 but remained a director until 1988, and kept close links with the building society which he built up and loved, until his death in 1997.* ***Below:*** *This Victorian building in Post Office Terrace was the society's home since 1861.*

In the days when many newly wed couples lived their early married lives sharing a house with in-laws building societies, such as the Cambridge Building Society, opened the road to liberty. Young men and women who were already investors were highly regarded as prospective mates

by the society which remained tenants of Christ's College until 1967. Since then the Cambridge Building Society, as it became known in 1945, has, more fittingly, been an owner-occupier rather than a tenant!

Further offices were opened in Fordham, Huntingdon and the cathedral city of Ely. Borrowers were then, in the main, prospective owner-occupiers attracted by the opportunity of owning their own homes for little more than the cost of renting them. The society also made loans to landlords, such as the canny bricklayer, and those wishing to start or expand factories and shops.

It had not been unusual in the days when cottage industrialists were their own masters for them to indulge so heavily at weekends that the habit of worshipping 'St Monday' arose. This allowed them an extra day's rest to recover from unwise drinking bouts after which they worked all hours to complete 'pieces' for sale on Saturday. Such conduct was an anathema to employers who required a sober workforce of regular habits to tend their machines. Local firms, which recognised the benefits of lifelong thrift and sobriety, encouraged staff to contribute part of their wages into the Cambridgeshire Permanent Benefit Building Society. It has always been recognised that family responsibilities usually turn wild young men into valuable members of the community.

while the wiser pairs opened joint accounts as soon as courtship took on a serious aspect. Wedding plans were often delayed until sufficient had been saved to pay for the house deposit and the society's branch manager had given his blessing on the requested mortgage. These conditions were still common in the 1950s and 60s. Marriage then was, of necessity, a difficult and serious undertaking quite different to the easier lending conditions prevailing in these more prosperous times.

Throughout the twentieth century the Cambridge Building Society has remained a local investment base for people to whom the Stock Exchange is an alarming mystery. Wide demographic investment in bricks and mortar is an uniquely Anglo-Saxon phenomenon widely practised in the English speaking world but unusual on the Continent. Europeans, and Scots, have a centuries old tradition of living in large tenement blocks where rents decrease as one struggles to the upper floors. The

Above: In 1981, Sawston was the first village to get its own branch of the Cambridge Building Society which operated from a portacabin while the present branch was being built. *Below:* The Board of Directors and Executive Managers in 1996.

estates of inter-war housing built on green fields around Cambridge, and all other English towns, were ultimately financed by mortgage borrowers. The speculative builders of the inter-war twenties and thirties and, later, of the post war years often enjoyed a sellers' market catering for the needs of 'a property owning democracy'.

During the Second World War the majority of 'Hostilities Only' servicemen called up for the duration of the war had a cash income worth, on average, one third of their pre-war earnings. Even the marriage allowances paid to wives of those who made over around one half of

their pay to their spouses did not permit the continuance of full pre-war premiums to building societies. The Cambridge, like many others, suffered from six years of underpayment of monthly repayments by borrowers in uniform. In 1940 the Hon Sec of the National Federation of Building Societies concluded that HM Government was not prepared to assist by subsidising repayments although the Secretary of State had implied that such might be the case. In other areas, not least the proliferation of airfields in the county's flat landscape, civilian workers enjoyed a prosperous war which gave them an unprecedented standard of living. As there was little to spend it on the wiser spirits saved with the Cambridge Building Society for the better years to come, let alone for a rainy day.

In 1945 members agreed to altered interest rates on shares, deposits and mortgages. The first prospectus of

the new era bore the old Victorian title 'Every man his own Landlord', a dream that rapidly became reality. Thanks to pegged rents and increased costs many private landlords found owning rentable property had changed from a way of producing a steady income to become an undesirable millstone. The society made loans to many sitting tenants privileged to buying at favoured prices when landlords got rid of property which had become a liability. During the years when local councils too enabled their tenants to purchase council houses at attractive prices the Cambridge Building Society also played its part in expanding the stake holding population.

which had to be replaced by larger models in 1993 and again in 1997. Such has been the rate of expansion thanks to public trust in the abilities of the growing Cambridge Building Society to invest depositors' funds wisely that all the administration has been moved to Newmarket Road. Here in the former home of the Cambridge Evening News are housed the main frame computer and the staff who have room for future development. Currently plans are in hand for further branches to be opened throughout the society's catchment area. As throughout its history the society continues to enable home owners and local businesses alike to realise their dreams, while at the same time contributing to the local economy and playing a key role in the local community.

In 1967 the society bought the former Cambridge Co-op premises, whose tenants had included a fishmongers and a tea room, which caused some comment both from citizens and the local press. Ten years later the Cambridge Building Society set about a programme of expansion so that 21 branches now cater for the convenience of members living in and around the Cambridge area. During the 1990s this programme succeeded in restoring branches in Ely and St Ives, Soham, St Neots and Huntingdon. Both Newmarket, the thriving centre of the valuable racing industry, and a number of residential villages such as Sawston and Burwell for example now provide full facilities for members.

As part of its modernisation plans the society first computerised members' accounts in 1975 with a system

Above: Cambridge Building Society staff make a presentation to the Arthur Rank Hospice and Day Care Appeal. Below: The society moved to its new Administration Centre in July 1997. The new headquarters stand on the site formerly occupied by the Cambridge News. The official opening was in March 1998 and was attended by the then Mayor of Cambridge, Daphne Roper maintaining a mayoral tradition by attending the CBS opening. One of her predecessors was in the chair for the society's inaugural meeting back in 1850.

From singing birds to water baths

The ingenious mechanical singing birds shown on TV antique programmes such as 'Going for a Song' may seem to have little connection with controlled environmental equipment for laboratories but many a business has its own unique story. In the case of Grant Instruments of Barrington and Shepreth, founder Peter Ward's interest in repairing such treasured antiques led to a job with a Cambridge company. In 1951, Festival of Britain Year, the young Olympic three-miler set up his own manufacturing business making laboratory water baths.

The unlikely venue for his scientific enterprise was the garden folly of the Old Vicarage at Grantchester known to the poet Rupert Brooke, who described Grantchester as 'the essence of Englishness'. Laboratory water baths provide a stable temperature for chemical and biological samples in much the same way as 'bains-maries' are used by cooks. Peter Ward developed one in which the hot water was stirred by fans under a false bottom so that the delicate chemical processes would not suffer from uneven heating. He also made his water baths with a detachable bridge of working parts which could be easily returned for 'swift two day' servicing, ideas since copied by many rivals.

The original vitreous enamelled and steel baths were superseded by stainless steel, and in 1954 the founder was joined by Cecil Chapman, physicist-cum-historian who had served in the Royal Navy as a radar officer. By 1957 Grant (from Grantchester) Instruments moved into the former corn mill at Barrington where John Barker, now the managing director, joined the firm as a part -time employee. Grant's reputation for innovation, quality and reliability led to increasing orders which by 1961 provided employment for six local full time staff.

Peter Ward, as an inventor, formed Grant Instruments (Developments) Ltd to continue research into the connected fields of thermistor thermometers and temperature recorders. A new factory, built to order, was opened in Shepreth in 1967 to which were moved sheet metal work, refrigeration engineering and final assembly work. The range of new products in the 1960s read like a laboratory suppliers catalogue offering new products such as dry block heaters, as an alternative to Bunsen burners. Other innovations included shaking water baths, which would keep the

Below: *The original 1951 Grant water bath.*
Bottom: *Bulbeck Mill, Barrington.*

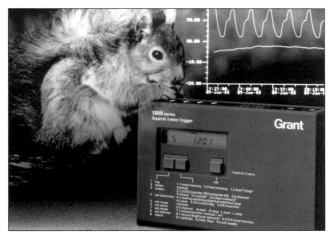

contents of flasks moving as well as the surrounding water.

The impetus given to school science teaching by the Nuffield project led to Grant producing a simple, thermostatic water bath. This mass produced polypropylene JB1 gave unsophisticated reliability for an outlay, in 1963, of £12-10s-0d (£12.50p). After repairing 100 year old singing birds the development, in the mid-1970s, of the solid state recording devices provided the modern world with highly efficient data recorders operating on up to fifty channels. The 1979 model solid-state memory recorder proved a boon to energy management and building industries because it could both store information for further processing and use it for separate display during research programmes.

The development of microprocessor technology Grants designed 'Squirrel' meter/loggers for a

diversity of uses in agriculture and transport, laboratory research and the conveyor ovens used in the food, china and other industries. Over 25,000 Grant Squirrels have been in use in the last two decades in extreme conditions ranging from the University Boat Race to the 6000M (19,000 feet) high weather stations on a glacier in the Tien Shan mountains. Customers' monitoring requirements vary from the complex electronics banks in nuclear submarines, via racing cars to the Virgin Challenger gas balloon. Squirrels are also used in scientific projects as diverse as investigating 'cot deaths' amongst human babies and experimental monitoring in the 'Space Station' in orbit around planet Earth.

When Peter Ward retired in 1979 his company was merged again with Grant Instruments. Exports account for 45 percent of sales enhanced by literature in many languages. A joint venture with a US Company YSI in the early 1990s led to the development of a water quality monitor to help combat pollution.

In 1998 an alliance with Boekel Scientific Inc has provided access to the US market for Grant products and given greater access to the life science market in Europe. Peter and Cecil's beliefs are the mainstay of the Company policy and today the firm provides employment for more than 100 people in a rural area. Grant continues to provide its customers with the best products in their field backed by their well known 'Speed of Service' so vital to laboratory management.

Above left: *A squirrel datalogger.* ***Top:*** *An example of today's laboratory equipment.*

1-2-3 years and still counting

He may have been a young whippersnapper of 24 years of age when it all began 123 years ago, but Charles Kidman is 'Great Grandad' to the Kidman family to-day. That tells you something about this family firm. Those blood ties and the sense of history has made this firm of building contractors more than just a business. It is one with the human touch, that values greatly the satisfaction of its clients.

You do not stay in business in the building trade if the words 'cowboy' or 'jerry-builder' become attached to you. To last and prosper for over a century, this can never have been the case with this firm of building contractors. Kidman & Sons Ltd has always been a family business valuing greatly the skill, ability and loyalty of all its workforce. It is justly proud that no job is too small to be disregarded and, whatever its size or relative importance, will receive the same professional and personal response as the larger contracts the company carries out. In a turbulent and unpredictable world most commercial concerns have a period of vigour, but the energy wanes and eventually they die or are absorbed by other newer organisations. A small number of companies survive more than one economic cycle and such is Kidman & Sons with a proud record of well over a century of service to the community. How did it all start?

Great grandad Charles was a bricklayer who launched his own business in 1876. What a time he chose. We all know of the recession of the 1990s and the depression of the 1930s. In Victorian times, they had their own version and it was well under way in the 1870s. But, with a dogged determination and a will to survive and prosper, by the time the 20th century dawned he had built most of the distinctive terraced houses in the Romsey area of Cambridge. On the back of this success, large contracts rolled in and he was able to retire from the trade before he had reached 45. You thought that early retirement was a modern idea. As with much else in life,

Above: Charles Kidman, 1852-1936, Founder of the Company. Below: A view of the original works in Sturton Street in 1894.

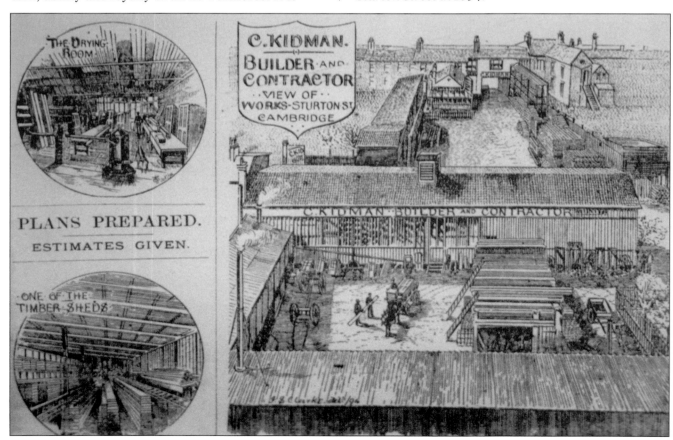

Today, 123 years after its foundation, Kidman & Sons is a smaller, but still thriving business with much experience to draw on. At the helm is another Charles Kidman, son of Eric, a fourth generation member. Together with his wife Annie as Company Secretary, and his uncle Colin, as chairman, he is determined to maintain the family tradition of personal service coupled with flexibility. To maintain this aim, with fewer family members involved, the business now takes on less large contracts but has expanded in the small works and maintenance market. This development, together with the works it has always carried out for the University, the Cambridge Colleges and other local institutions, has

Charles not only thought of it first, but did it. All four of Charles' sons were involved in running the company over the next 40 years. During this period, Heffer's Printing Works, which became the home of Radio Cambridge, the University Arms Hotel and the Cambridgeshire Waterworks depot were built. After the Second World War, under the guidance of cousins Colin, Jack and Eric, Kidman & Sons continued to expand its business, though the total number of employees had peaked at 200 in 1938. In 1943 the firm moved to its present address in Victoria Road and has recently moved into newly furbished offices on the same site.

ensured continued success. From the office, workshops and yard in Victoria Road, skilled operatives of all trades are on hand for the craft of building. However small the task, clients can expect, and get, the service that the Kidman family has given for each and every one of those 123 years.

Above: *Charles Kidman, the present Managing Director, flanked by his late father Eric, and his uncle Colin, the present chairman, at a party in 1991 to make long service presentations to members of staff.*
Top: *The Company's newly refurbished offices on part of their extensive site in Victoria Road.*

A modern hotel in Victorian surroundings

Absorb the air of Victorian elegance around the Arundel House Hotel and you are back over a century ago when the horses and carriages hustled and bustled their way along Chesterton Road. The hotel's period facade has been carefully preserved to remind visitors of the days when noble steeds pulled up outside to offload the occupants of the shining carriages they pulled. These prestigious houses, built between l870 and 1875, have been skilfully converted to form what is now the main hotel building. Tucked away behind the main building is the timber framed 'Coach House' which was originaIIy constructed for the Cambridge Omnibus Company in l894 The Omnibus Company was the first fee paying horse drawn carriage company to carry passengers in and around the city. What is now referred to as the Coach House was really the stables, with the carriages at the rear and the loft above being used for storage of hay and tack. The clip clop of the hooves and the sparking of the horses shoes on the cobbles and flagstones did not last for long. The dreaded motorised vehicles were waiting just round the corner of the 20th century. After only a decade the stables were no longer needed as the Omnibus Company went out of business. The building had been put to split use by the 1920s with a vehicle repair business, Frost's Garage, becoming established in one half while the other half saw a succession of small industrial firms come and

Right: The 'Coach House' built in 1894 for Cambridge Omnibus Co. Below: A coach and pair in Chesterton High Street. The horses would have been stabled in what the hotel now calls the 'Coach House'.

go over the decades until 1981 when the last industrial occupant,Wire Design, sold their half to the by now rapidly expanding Arundel House Hotel.

The creation of a hotel on this site was the brainchild of John Douglas Norfolk. As a Major in the army Royal Signals he had served in Hong Kong, developing the telecommunications set up over there in the 1950s. Back home, as an electrical engineer, the 'Major' as he is still affectionately known to many, became a manager within the Pye Group of companies in Cambridge before deciding to branch out into the hotel business. Already the owner of a number of residential properties in Cambridge, in 1970 he purchased No 61 Chesterton Road, a turret house at one end of the terrace, which opened the following year with just 12 bedrooms as the Arundel House Hotel. In the early years Mr Norfolk was fortunate to have the services of Peggy and Doug

bishments taking place every year throughout this period.

With its lovely views across the river Cam to the open parkland of Jesus Green the hotel has grown in under 30 years from a modest 12 bedrooms to its present total of 105, making it now the fourth largest hotel in the city. Whilst keeping up with modern trends in facilities and comfort, the Norfolk family have retained many Victorian features within the hotel with its elegant bar, award winning restaurant and magnificent Victorian style Conservatory and garden. The old stable masters cottage, much enlarged, is now a staff house and the re-introduction of cobblestones and Victorian style lamp posts in the BALI award winning resurfacing and landscaping of the car park has continued the theme. In 1999, as its 'Millennium' project, restoration of the whole exterior to the splendour of its past has begun, thus preserving the Victorian aura for future generations.

Above: The hotel frontage pictured in 1900 when the houses were known as Sentis Terrace. They were built between 1870 and 1875. Below: An aerial view of the hotel in its present guise.

Clark. He had known them at Pye and because of their knowledge of the hotel and guest house trade installed them as managers.

Small though it was the hotel proved to be a great success and a year later in 1972 work began to convert two properties further along the terrace, Nos 53 and 55, already owned by the Major and let as flats and bedsits. The early involvement at this stage of John Norfolk's son Robert, during the long summer school holiday working alongside the builders in the creation of the 'new' hotel was an early sign of things to come.

With the opening of 23 new bedrooms and a completely new bar, restaurant and kitchen, the original hotel became an annexe with the public areas converted to extra bedrooms bringing the total number of rooms to 38. During the 70s further properties fortuitously came on the market and the main building and annexe eventually merged into a continuous row of five out of the nine houses in the complete terrace.

In 1981, with retirement approaching for Peggy and Doug Clark, Robert Norfolk, who by then had completed a Bsc Hons degree at Surrey University in Hotel and Catering Management and had earned his spurs in the trade as a trainee manager at the world renowned Dorchester Hotel in London followed by Assistant and Deputy Manager positions within Trusthouse Forte, joined the family business as General Manager, assuming the full mantle of Managing Director on the departure of the Clarks.

Robert Norfolk's first project was the conversion of the first half of the Coach House purchased in 1981, followed by another house in the terrace, No 51, in 1984, the other half of the Coach House acquired from Frost Garage in 1987 and two more houses in the early 1990s, with other improvements and refur-

A new car and 'divi' too

Which came first, the chicken or the egg? Which was established first in Cambridge, the Co-operative Retail services or Herbert Robinson Ltd? Both seem to have been with us since the year dot, but it is the Co-op that can claim the record of being first to arrive. The Co-operative movement had begun in the Lancashire mill town of Rochdale, in 1844. A group of poor weavers pooled their meagre resources and bought their goods together at a discounted bulk rate. Selling on to others, from the little shop on Toad Lane, customers could become members. Surplus profits were distributed and each member guaranteed a dividend - the famous Co-op 'divi'. The idea quickly spread through Britain and arrived in Cambridge in 1869 at 8 City Road. It was not until 1903 that Herbert Robinson Senior began trading.

However, the Co-operative movement and the future of Robinson's would be linked, however unlikely it appeared at that time. Even in 1908, there was the No 1 branch of the Co-op on Mill Road. By the end of the 20th century, the head offices of Herbert Robinson Ltd were situated on the very same road. The style and size of the premises are, however, rather different. In the mid 1960s, the Cambridge Co-operative Society bought Robinson's. It was merged in turn with the CRS in 1990. As such, Herbert Robinson Ltd is a wholly owned subsidiary. It has been a long journey from that little shop in East Lancashire to the giant that has developed over 150 years further on. Those early Pioneers would have never heard of the motor car, much less Homeworld and Living, that are part of the retail trade these days. As the Co-op has diversified into non-food

as well as food outlets, the opportunity to bring members the advantages of more varied buying in bulk has given them the benefits of cheaper and more attractive shopping. Not a lot of people, including Michael Caine, know that there are over 50 independent retail societies under the same umbrella. When you add in the Insurance Society, Bank, Travel and Wholesale Society that all share the Co-operative name, then you realise the mammoth nature of the group. Despite its size, the CRS clings firmly to the moral preached to those early Cambridge Co-op workers, back in Victorian times. They were told to work hard, treat each other with respect and always strive to give value for money. You would find it hard to quarrel with that instruction in any era.

For Herbert Robinson, life did not flow quite as smoothly in his first days in business in the city. In 1903, he became the manager of the Premier Cycle Company that traded from a depot in Cambridge. The venture struggled to make ends meet to such a degree that it folded two years later. Mr Robinson felt that there was an opportunity for him to turn things around with his own brand of vision and planning. His former employers were helpful in lending him the princely sum of £50. With that, and other credit facilities they arranged, he was able to buy the business. Renamed 'Robinson's Bicycle Showrooms', it flourished. So much so, that he was able to open two other depots within the next few years. It was his next move that showed his foresight. In 1909 he acquired a depot on Green Street, from where he sold motor cycles. The coming of the age of the horseless carriage was overlooked by some as a passing fad. Herbert had more sense. He extended the premises and, by the time the Great War came along, he had been appointed as a distributor for Singer and Hillman. It was with those makers of cars, with such later distinctive names as Minx, Imp, Hawk and Snipe, that the company was to have long connections. Lord Rootes, then Sir Reginald, performed the opening ceremony when more new premises were opened on Regent Street in 1932. The garages, showrooms and workshops occupied 40,000 sq ft. It must have seemed light years away from the little bike shop where it had all begun. From 1935, all the Rootes Group products were to be handled by Herbert Robinson Ltd.

Above: *The old Honda site on Coldhams Lane which is now the Mazda dealership.* **Left:** *A staff outing during the 1950s.*

Herbert Robinson Ltd has many outlets in Cambridge and Bedford. It is a sign of the times that many of these distribute cars which had their origins abroad. The names of Nissan, Honda, Fiat and Mazda sit side by side in Bedford and those of Alfa Romeo, Fiat and Suzuki have now joined the likes of Honda and Mazda in Cambridge now that the former Frank Holland Motors on Mill Road have been taken over. Not that this

Success breeds success. This was well illustrated as things gathered a-pace after World War II. Confirmed franchises helped finalise plans for further development. In 1956, a Shell Service Station was opened on the A10. As well as an accessory shop, it offered a car valeting service. This was virtually unheard of in the days when you took a bucket, sponge and, if you were lucky, a brush to the car's coachwork and upholstery. This was another example of the Robinson Company thinking ahead. Shortly afterwards, the 200 ft frontage of another new site appeared on the Newmarket Road. By the late 1950s, there was a 24 hour breakdown service, drive through car wash and a department store on Regent Street, selling radios, televisions and other electrical goods. Just to remember the links with the old days, you could buy a new drop-handled racing bike there, as well. The company has always been up to date with its advertising as well as its service and product delivery. The care hire facility was accompanied by the phrase 'Drive in style for less per mile'. It was already aware of the power of the snappy slogan.

has made much difference to what the company stands for. The aim of providing quality motoring backed by a quality service remains unabashed. As the motoring division of the CRS, Herbert Robinson was formed into a separate company, with Brian Pettengell as managing director, in the early 1990s. Still looking to expand and provide greater choice and variety for its customers, the Cecil & Larter (Fiat) was the latest to have come under the company wing. It was acquired on 29 May 1999. Ee by gum, those old weavers and cotton workers oop in Lancashire would have been proud of the way the pooling of resources has been taken on in the Cambridge motor trade. They would also have approved of the way the CRS and Robinson's have combined their talents for the benefit of shareholder and public like. In many cases, they are the one and the same.

Above: *The Honda Dealership on Newmarket Road, Cambridge.* ***Top:*** *The Mazda Dealership on Coldhams Lane*

A racing certainty for "Excellence in Engineering"

George Lister was a proud and God fearing man who believed that if job was worth doing, then it was a righteous thing to do it well. A learned man, despite leaving school at the age of ten, he read widely and educated himself with lengthy study at night school. He had a quick, mathematical brain and could do the sort of mental arithmetic that would leave cold those of us educated in the 'like it or leave it' style of teaching of recent years. He knew the Bible from cover to cover and was a frequent preacher at the Baptist Chapel.

He was also the founder of a business partnership that became George Lister & Sons Ltd. Not only is it one of the longest established companies in Cambridge, but it is also one of the most famous. That worldwide fame originates from the fifty Lister sports racing cars his grandson Brian designed and the company built in the 1950s. These cars with MG, Bristol, Maserati, Jaguar and Chevrolet engines have won races and championships all over the world and it is estimated that those fifty original cars have won or been placed two thousand times, which must constitute some kind of record, an average of forty places per car!

The tradition of success with Lister cars continues into the 90s with the name being used under licence on the winning Lister 'Storm' cars produced in Leatherhead.

The story behind these achievements is most interesting and all part of the history of Cambridge. George Lister started the company as a partnership in 1890. He was a skilled machinist and engineer and his partners were two blacksmiths, Charles Flatters and Harry Branch. They quickly drew in

Left: George Lister 1858 - 1930. **Below:** *Cambridge MP-to-be Robert Rhodes James, left, with Brian Lister and Mrs Margaret Thatcher, the then leader of the Opposition, in a Lister Jaguar at the factory in Cherry Hinton in the late 1970s.* **Bottom:** *The Abbey Road offices and factory entrance circa 1948.*

servicing work from local companies, it must be remembered that in Victorian England most supplies had to be produced locally, therefore dairies, bakeries, gas producers, water companies were all based in the city and their mechanical equipment had to be installed and serviced.

By the turn of the twentieth century, Lister's were firmly established in Cambridge as service engineers, keeping the city's industry running smoothly. By 1920 both partners had retired and George Lister's sons, Alfred and Horace, had been brought in to help run the concern, now employing fifteen people. Its title was now George Lister & Sons. Alfred had ambitions about specialising in the rapidly increasing motor car market, but it was not to be, he died late in that decade.

On the death of George Lister, his younger son, Horace, turned the company into a limited liability company. Horace and his wife, Nell, became directors. The skills of the company were expanding in various directions. As an example, their blacksmithing shop was producing high quality architectural metal work, the railings between the Senate House and Kings College front lawn are a Lister product and from that vantage point on King's Parade you can also observe the weather vanes on Kings dining hall, another product of the company, as are the lanterns on the Senate House.

Horace Lister saw to it that his company was the first in Cambridge to offer a mobile arc welding service, the welders going to the customers' site, very enterprising in the early 30s.

Horace and Nell Lister had two sons, Raymond and Brian, both of whom joined the company as apprentices and after gaining their experience as improvers they eventually became directors. Raymond specialising in architectural metal work, the company at this time restoring some of the

finest pieces of wrought iron in the U K. Bakewell's Arbour for instance, at Melbourne Hall in Derbyshire. Lister's made the entrance gates for the Perse School on Hills Road in Cambridge. This was the school that Brian had attended. He served his apprenticeship during the war and after national service in the RAF returned with high ambitions for developing Listers machine shop and he also introduced a sheet metal section into the business. He had had a lifelong interest in motor cars, like his uncle Alfred, but in Brian's case this had been frustrated by wartime restrictions on motoring. Now on his return in 1948 he could give it his full attention. This began with modifying existing cars and then building 'specials'. It was at this time that he was to meet another competitor who was to help him bring fame to the Lister name.

He was Archie Scott Brown, a young Scot living in Cambridge, dreadfully disabled, born without a right hand and very deformed legs and feet but he was a genius at the wheel of competition cars. They formed a team and were joined by Don Moore, also like Brian, born in Cambridge and a highly skilled engine development specialist.

The story of the team, supported by the skills of George Lister & Sons Ltd. is a motor racing legend. Winning the first race they entered with the Lister M.G. in 1954, they went on to win classics like the 1955 British Empire Trophy in a Lister Bristol and again in 1957 with a Lister Jaguar. In that year they won eleven races entered out of fourteen, humbling the mighty Aston Martin team

Above: The award winning book Archie and the Listers by Robert Edwards, published by Patrick Stephens Ltd.
Below: The Abbey Road machine shop in the 1920s. The craftsman in the centre of the picture is Freddie Benstead who served the company for 65 years.

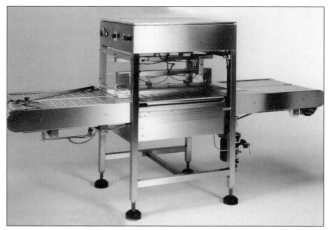

on all but one occasion that year. Archie was tragically killed at Spa in Belgium in 1958. This story of heroics and enterprise is told in the award winning book 'Archie and the Listers' by Robert Edwards published in 1995 which had ecstatic reviews in the motoring press. One American journalist described it as 'the best book on motor racing I have ever read'. In the UK the Autocar listed it as one of the ten 'must have' books to begin a library on motoring.

The Lister Jaguar itself has been described by Walter Hayes, President of Aston Martin Lagonda as A National Treasure", marvellous praise from what had been a principal rival. The list of drivers of Listers reads like a "Who's Who of Racing Motorists". Apart from Archie Scott Brown, there was Stirling Moss, Jim Clark, Roy Salvadori, Ivor Bueb, Innes Ireland, and Americans, Briggs Cunningham and Caroll Shelby and more recently Tiff Needell, Tony Dron, Gary Pearson, Frank Sytner and the American Syd Silverman who once owned 'Variety' magazine but decided to go motor racing instead. Brian is very proud that Syd owns five of the fifty cars produced. The cars are still performing and winning in historic races all over the world. This years tally adding at least another twenty five successes to the total.

Now what of the company since the glory days of the 1950s.

Thirty years ago, Lister's moved to an industrial estate on Coldhams Lane, Cherry Hinton. Raymond Lister retired some years ago selling his shares to Brian and two new directors, Martin Murray and Malcolm Webdale, both long established Lister employees.

The intention is that eventually they will buy Brian's shares so that the future of the company is assured. The company has a marvellous employment record having retired several craftsmen with fifty years service, another who continued on a part time basis clocked up sixty five years. In these days of early retirement, thirty years is looked upon as normal at Lister's. Brian Lister himself is approaching his fifty eighth year of service. The company is still on the same Cherry Hinton industrial park it moved to thirty years ago but is now in another factory opened in 1997 appropriately enough by Stirling Moss.

Today they produce complete electronically controlled food packaging and loading machines which are exported to many countries and have to meet the stringent regulations of the European Community and the U.S. Authorities. Special purpose machines used in the production of plastic sheet and film is another example of the capital equipment they manufacture. They are in addition currently making cabinets to house TV transmitters for another of their customers and they also make the metal parts that are used in transmitting the analogue and digital signals from these transmitter units. Various departments of the University are amongst their customers as are many of the hi-tech specialist companies formed by young Cambridge entrepreneurs who have the same urge to serve the community that George Lister had 109 years ago in his quest for 'Excellence in Engineering' which is Lister's maxim!

Above: *An electronically controlled stainless steel food packaging machine typical of Lister's products today.*
Top: *Oulton Park Empire Trophy, 1958. Archie Scott Brown, Lister Jaguar, leads Bruce Halford, Lister Jaguar, a D-type Jaguar and an Aston Martin off the line.* ***Inset:*** *Archie Scott Brown.*

Exhibitionists to industry

The attractive conservation area of Histon's Village Green makes an appropriate setting for Korten Limited, a company which specialises in displaying products and services to their best advantage. Korten occupies a handsome 19th century building which served first as the Village Institute, then as an apple store for Chivers, before falling into disuse. In the early 60s it was given a new lease of life when it was taken over and renovated by Korten, a young exhibition design and production company based, prior to their move, in Shelley Row, Cambridge. The company was moreover eminently well-qualified to carry out the restoration and conversion of this fine, historic structure, as one of its founders was the son of the local painting contractors R C Starling & Son.

G C Starling had left the family business to branch out on his own, and in 1960, together with co-founder K Fawcett, he established Korten Limited, offering imaginative designs for the exhibition industry and also providing a professional construction service. Since then, two more generations of the Starling family have followed the founder into the business, working alongside their skilled staff and consistently coming up with the effective, original concepts that have attracted and held an impressive and ever-growing list of clients, from the small local businesses to blue-chip organisations. Companies in such varied sectors of industry as pharmaceutical, scientific and lifestyle have successfully marketed their products with the help of Korten's professional expertise. In some ways the world of the exhibition-designer is similar to that of the film-producer and the stage-setter. Unlike the two latter, though, the Korten staff produce practical, functional settings in which the exhibitors and their visitors can conduct business in comfort. Typical exhibition stands contain display counters, desks, small store rooms and large display panels for photographs and

sales messages; some may be ornamented by tall advertising towers or enhanced by video screens and other audio-visual displays; in fact, they can be as ornate or as simple as the client wishes. It is normal for the decorative finishes which cover the wood 'skeleton' to be finished in the corporate colours of the stand holder, and the logo will generally feature prominently; but beyond that clients rely on Korten's creativity and craftsmanship to devise ways of promoting their company image when all around, in crowded exhibition halls, other exhibitors are working in competition to attract customers' eyes. They are never disappointed; working from their brief, Korten will complete the entire project at a competitive price. At exhibitions at home or abroad, Korten originality and quality is the key to its own - and its customers' - continuing success.

Below: *Gordon Starling, James Pace MP and Terry Howard view an exhibition design.*
Bottom: *One of Korten's recent exhibitions.*

Setting the pace from valve wireless to mobile communications

The firm which was to achieve worldwide acclaim as Pye Radio Ltd, subsequently becoming Philips and more recently Simoco International Limited, was originally set up in 1896 by William George Pye in a shed in the garden of the family home in Humberstone Road, Chesterton. The following year the business moved to 30 St Andrews Street, relocating a short time afterwards to the Granta Works in Mill Lane where it was to remain for 14 years, growing all the while.

The firm's next move took it to Cam Road. By now it was employing 40 people, and war was imminent. Soon the firm was producing specialist precision instruments for military use, including Hartree Height Finders for aeroplanes, gun-sights, special telescopes, Aldis Signalling Lamps and resistance boxes used to measure the circuits in mines.

In 1920 an employee named George Ceadel made a wireless set. The company immediately recognised the significance of this achievement and concentrated on the exciting new phenomenon of wireless, developing a series of educational kits primarily for use in schools and colleges, but which also became popular with radio amateurs.

National broadcasting was launched in 1922 to an eager welcome from a large audience. Pye began producing its 520, 530, 540 and 550 series of receivers - the latter with a magnificent horn-type loudspeaker - followed in 1924 by the very successful 720, 730 and 749. The following year the first Pye Portable Receiver came into mass production. The famous Rising Sun motif which some readers will remember first began to appear on loudspeaker cabinets in 1927 and was to remain a feature throughout the early 30s, making a final appearance on Pye Model M78F in 1948.

Below: *Pye RTC (Radio Telephone Controller).*
Bottom: *Pye Service Van.*

In 1928 the Pye family sold the radio-manufacturing side of the business and moved to new premises on Newmarket Road where they continued as instrument makers, and the following year Charles Orr Stanley, the new owner, registered his company as Pye Radio Ltd. Having watched Baird's early experiments with television with interest, Pye began work to develop its own television receivers, and its models were amongst the first on the market when the BBC introduced its service in 1936. Three years later Pye turned to the war effort again, setting up its first Radiolocation (Radar) station at Walton-on-Naze to detect approaching enemy, and going on to develop a succession of high-precision devices including a range Radar devices to improve the accuracy of our bombs, while the Pye Proximity Fuse for use in anti-aircraft shells was regarded as one of the outstanding war-time developments.

The early post-war years saw a succession of improvements - many of them pioneered by Pye - in the quality of television sets, resulting in more reliable and more compact sets with clearer pictures with less interference. For years the Pye B16T television set was regarded as the best on the market, while a more fleeting interest was aroused by the first public demonstration of 3D television - again by Pye; and the company was involved in developments in a whole range of novel televisual applications, including CCTV, underwater television, aircraft landing systems, stereo and high-fidelity audio reproduction, and the introduction of the transistorised portable in 1956.

Above left: *Pye Bantam - one of the first portable radios.* ***Above right:*** *London policeman using a motorcycle radio.*

Innovation continued, although the management of the company changed; Pye merged with E K Cole Limited (Ekco) in 1960 to form British Electronic Industries Limited, was subsequently renamed Pye of Cambridge Limited and was taken over in 1967 by the Dutch Philips Group. When colour television was launched on 1st July 1967, VIPs at the London Hilton watched the event on Pye television sets. More recently Pye, as part of Philips, led the way in audio-visual and telecommunication innovations such as VCR technology, Teletext and Viewdata.

Since 1st July 1996 the company's contributions to the field of modern radio communications have continued under its new name of Simoco International Limited (an acronym for Systems Integration and Mobile Communications); this company was formed through the acquisition of Philips Telecom - Private Mobile Radio from Philips Electronics, and is backed by venture capitalists CINVen. Focusing on the buoyant global radio communications market, Simoco has all the necessary skills and resources to stay at the forefront of its field, and will provide new solutions, products and technologies to keep pace with customers' rapidly-changing needs and maintain its leading position in the development of TETRA (TErrestrial Trunked RAdio) digital mobile radio.

Developing and bringing new technologies to market is not an easy task, especially when conducted on an international scale. In 1989 the Company started work on TETRA, a new digital radio technology, which is the equivalent in the mobile communications field to the change from audio tape to the compact disc. Since that time Simoco has been at the forefront of developing the TETRA standard through ETSI, the European Telecommunications Standards Institute, and working through the technological challenges to bring its first products to market in 1998.

Along the way Simoco achieved a number of significant milestones. In 1995 the Company produced the first demonstrator, to prove the viability of the technology, and two years later was the first to demonstrate two way telephone calls on a public safety style handportable. In 1998 Simoco shipped the first working TETRA system for use in a public safety application in the UK to West Midlands Ambulance Service.

Simoco was also invited, that year, to take over the Chairmanship of an International Association of industry and user organisations known as the TETRA MoU Association. This honour was largely in recognition of its leading role in technology innovation and its activities in marketing and promoting the new standard. In this capacity Simoco led delegations to China and the USA.

Simoco has set itself the goal of working with customers to deliver the most dependable mobile communications solutions, and it works closely with end users, consultants and contractors to study each new challenge and to meet it through the provision of either standard or custom-built systems. Radio communication has always been an exciting area to be involved in, as first Pye and then Philips discovered; and as we move into the next millennium, it will be Simoco which not only responds to the needs of its markets, but sets the pace.

Left: TETRA handportable in action at West Midlands Ambulance. Below: Simoco's head office in Cambridge.

No stony reception from the 'Warmer Company'

It is all computers and virtual reality these days. There is no such thing as a time served master craftsman any more. No pride in his work and no attention to detail are common failings in the worker these days. If you listen to the prophets of doom, then that is what you will believe. If you want to see the real world of the skilled professional, providing a quality service in a traditional craft, then you do not have far to travel. Come along to the show rooms and works on Newmarket Road and be prepared to eat your words. It is here that the family business of Ivett & Reed is based, close to the soccer ground that was the passion of 'Grandma' Elsie Reed. Monumental stonemasons since 1896, the company has kept and developed the skills that have made it a by-word in Cambridge. Through four generations of the Reed family, the lettering has been etched on carefully selected and polished stone to cater for the customer's every need.

Right: *Sam, Bernard and Victor Reed in a picture dating from the 1920s.*
Below: *Newmarket Road - 1904.*

As young men Fred Ivett and his cousin, Sam Reed, were apprentices at Saint's Masons. They took over the ownership on the retirement of Mr Saint. At first they occupied premises on Mill Road and Devonshire Road. The latter closed in 1902 and the head offices were then set up on Newmarket Road. Although the shop on Mill Road stayed within the firm until the 1970s, the business was consolidated at the Newmarket Road site in the 1920s. Mr Reed was the stonemason and Mr Ivett the letter cutter. They soon built a local reputation as reliable and gifted craftsmen. Not only were they proud of what they achieved, there was a great pleasure to be had in turning a drab piece of stone into something close to a work of art. With two horses, a donkey and a cart as backup, stone works were carted away to customers. It was not until the end of the Great War that an old Lawrence Panhard chain driven truck was bought. Mr Ivett died in 1922 and the depression years of the late 1920s and early 1930s bit hard. But, it was those with dedication and quality who survived the dark days. The Reeds, for by now Bernard had joined his father, had those attitudes. Those were the days of mixing by hand as concrete mixers were machines for the future. Bath stone was lifted to form bay windows and York stone laid for steps. Marble, rather than granite, was the popular material for decorative and memorial purposes. But, it was the natural English stones that were mainly used in the various elements of the masonry trade. Life was hard and the work tough, but great satisfaction was gained from a job well done. That thought has been passed down through

the successive generations of Sam, Bernard and David to the latest family member, Andrew.

Having come through the problems of those hard times, war came again in 1939 to take away some of Ivett & Reed's masons to serve King and country. It was hard to obtain materials and life was far from easy again. As ever, it was that attention to detail and doggedness in maintaining the high standards of workmanship that kept the family business afloat. As things settled on a more even keel, Ivett & Reed was able to return to the art of working stone. The finest Italian marble and natural materials were selected then, as now, to ensure that the product was top notch. When Andrew Reed joined the firm in 1982, the business was almost entirely made up of stonemasonry work and the preparation of memorials. He was able to help widen horizons, gradually shifting during the 80s to a more varied product. Now the company is one of the leading lights in the county in producing attractive and stylish fireplaces in granite and marble. So well known is it that it has a bus stop named after it in the official timetable! Kitchen worktops and vanity shelves are now sculpted with the same loving care as the other more traditional items. Ivett & Reed has even grasped the technological age with relish. Computerised diamond bladed saws, power tools and computerised memorial lettering have all come to rest happily alongside the traditional.

Above: *Mill Road in the early 1900s. Ivett & Reed's premises can be seen in the background.*

Building on the success of previous generations

Even as a little boy, the founder Robert George Carter knew what he wanted to be when he grew up - he wanted to be a carpenter, like his grandfather. And this was the first of many wise decisions which have led to the R G Carter Group becoming the successful, well-respected construction company that it is today.

Young George, as he chose to be called (George was his grandfather's name) became a carpenter's apprentice at the age of 14, practising his new skills with the tools he had inherited from his grandfather. After his apprenticeship he tried life in London, decided it was not for him, and returned to East Anglia, where he spent the next few years working alongside experienced craftsmen who displayed the high level of skill that was to become so important to George.

In 1914 George Carter joined up and served in France. His bravery, which almost cost him his life on a number of occasions, earned him the Military Medal and the Croix de Guerre. Within three days of being demobbed he found employment on a building site in Norwich; he quickly rose to foreman and then to general foreman, and by 1921 he was married and running his own business.

From the outset, the whole family was involved in the venture; his uncles helped him financially, his wife Florence acted as secretary, bookkeeper and wages clerk and her brother Ted drove the horse and trolley, and later the motor lorry. George worked tirelessly to get his business up and running, but always managed to find time for his children, Robert Edward, Betty, Mary and Ruth. Where work was concerned, his guiding rule was that a contract had to be completed on time even if it meant working from six in the morning until ten in the evening during the summer months. When a contract was finished he liked to put up hoardings emblazoned with the firm's proud boast, On Time Again!. He would not tolerate timewasters, but he would reward hard work, and this created great loyalty among his workforce.

Having survived the depression of the late 1920s and early 1930s, George decided in 1932 to turn the firm into a limited company. His son Bob joined R G Carter Limited as an

Below (both pictures): *The Maitland Robinson Library, constructed by RG Carter in 1992.*

apprentice carpenter six years later, but unfortunately his early career was interrupted, as his father's had been, by the outbreak of war. The firm obtained a steady stream of Government contracts; one of the more unusual jobs the construction of a fake city, complete with homes and factories, at Withernsea, as a decoy to draw German bombers away from nearby Hull.

Bob Carter returned in 1946, and took over as managing director in 1950. In the early 50s, under Bob Carter's leadership, business began to boom, and by the mid-1950s, R G Carter had become the largest building firm in Norfolk.

R G Carter's first contract in the City was the Pye building in the 1950s. Further contracts followed including some on the continuing development of Marshall's Airport, a relationship that is still maintained today. This included Hangar 17, built in 1982 as part of the Falklands War effort and at the time Europe's largest single span aircraft hangar; and more recently Marshall's Landrover and Jaguar car showrooms.

Other large contracts included the Tesco superstore site, created at Bar Hill in 1977 and the first of its kind in the area; the Bridge Street shops and offices development; and a major extension to the Anglia Polytechnic University.

Over the last 25 years the firm has also been privileged to carry out many prestigious contracts for the Cambridge University colleges. Among these are the Maitland Robinson Library at Downing College, the St John's College Library, the Rosalind Franklin Building at Newnham College, and the Library and Auditorium at Homerton College. Many of its buildings have been formally opened by royalty, the most recent being by HRH The Duke of Edinburgh, who unveiled new student accommodation and a Master's Lodge at Pembroke College in 1998. Part of this development, Foundress Court, also had the distinction of winning one of just four awards made in the eastern region by the Royal Institute of British Architects.

Another recent highlight was the 1998 opening of the Aoi Pavilion at Cambridge University Library. Sponsored by a Japanese businessman, it now houses a remarkable collection of Japanese and East Asian books and manuscripts.

In 1992 the company formally opened its office at Barnwell House, Barnwell Drive, Cambridge CB5 8UU (telephone 01223 414033).

The Group is currently enjoying the most successful period in its history under the chairmanship of Robert Carter, Bob's son. This family tradition, now in its third generation, is a crucial element in the stability and security of the workforce and the continued expansion and success of the company.

Above left: *Hangar 17 of Cambridge Airport, designed and built by RG Carter.* ***Top:*** *St John's College Library, Cambridge, completed in June 1993.*

Booking a place in history

Cambridge's students and other booklovers have by now grown accustomed to being able to browse at leisure around the Cambridge University Press Bookshop on Trinity Street. This convenient location has been the home of Cambridge University Press since 1992, but in fact books have been sold here since the 16th century, and it is believed to be the site of the oldest bookshop in the country - making it a most appropriate home for the world's oldest publisher.

The Press's first home was a printing house in Regent Walk, sited where the Senate House lawn now is, just opposite the bookshop. This was established following the granting of the Royal Charter by Henry VIII, which in 1534 gave the University the right to print, publish and sell books. The University's first printer was Thomas Thomas, and his grave, along with the graves of other University printers of that era, can be seen at the University Church. The Press's first book was printed in 1584, and since then the Press has been operating continuously as a printer and publisher to become one of the largest academic and educational publishers in the world.

Over the years it has published works by many famous scholars: Henry More, John Milton, Isaac Newton, Arthur Eddington, Steven Runciman, Quentin Skinner, John Dunn

and many, many more. During the mid 19th century the Press focused on the printing of Bibles and prayer books; in 1874 it started publishing school textbooks, and by the end of the century it had begun publishing journals. Both these areas remain strong today; teachers have continued to rely on the University Press's innovative and well-respected range of teaching materials from the very first Pitt Press schoolbooks to more recent courses such as *School Mathematics Project* or *Cambridge Latin Course*, while the *Journal of Physiology*, in 1893 the first journal to be launched by the Press, still ranks among the most successful journals alongside more recent introductions such as *Protein Science*, *Contemporary European History* and *English Today*. Other large-scale works for which Cambridge University Press is noted include the *Cambridge Modern History*, first published in 1902, followed by more than 25 similar series; the Cambridge Encyclopedia family; the scholarly editions of D H Lawrence and Joseph Conrad; the *Darwin Correspondence*; and the *Mathematical Papers of Isaac Newton*. Less weighty publications include the highly successful *Cambridge Reading* series for youngsters, local interest books, the popular 'Canto' series, and thousands of academic monographs and professional books. English language acquisition is one of the specialist areas well

Below: *The Cambridge University Press Bookshop.*

covered by the Press, and its English Language Teaching programme is widely used in language colleges today.

Cambridge University Press has a worldwide reputation for attracting the best authors and publishing the best work in the English language. Statisticians may like to know that the Press has over 24,000 authors in 108 countries, publishes over 2400 separate publication units a year which are sold to more than 190 countries across the globe, and has more than 14,000 books in print, along with maps, wall-charts, slides, cards, disks and CDs. All the new Cambridge publications and the whole backlist of more than 12,500 titles are, as far as possible, kept permanently on display and available for sale at the Press Bookshop, where visitors can browse happily in the calm, friendly atmosphere, and where staff are always on hand to offer advice and information, not only on the full range of titles but also on forthcoming University and city events.

The Bookshop itself is of great architectural interest and has a very distinguished history. It was occupied by bookseller William Scarlet in 1851 to 1617, then it changed hands 11 times before being acquired in 1845 by Daniel and Alexander Macmillan (the former, incidentally, was Harold Macmillan's grandfather). During this era the Bookshop seems to have become something of a club for Daniel Macmillan's many

friends at the University, and enjoyed visits from great literary figures such as Tennyson, Thackeray and Charles Kingsley. When Alexander Macmillan moved to London in 1863 to manage the Macmillan publishing business the Bookshop was taken over by his nephew Robert Bowes and became first Macmillan & Bowes, then Bowes & Bowes. Bowes & Bowes was acquired by W H Smith in 1953, and in 1986 the Bookshop became part of the W H Smith-owned Sherratt & Hughes chain.

By 1991 the building was in need of reconstruction and refurbishment. The splendid facade, with its elegant 19th century windows, was restored and cleaned, and the door replaced in its earlier position. Many original features were uncovered during reconstruction, and these have been restored and incorporated into the overall design: Tudor beams on the ground floor, decorative cast-iron Victorian columns with lotus-leaf capitals, and a delicate plaster cornice with lotus and acanthus foliage on the first floor. Following the refurbishment the Press Bookshop was opened in 1992. There is so much of interest in both the building and its contents that a visit to the Press Bookshop is sure to prove a fascinating experience.

Above: *The Edinburgh Building, headquarters of the Press's Publishing Division.*

This ice cream seller, believed to be Arthur Mayes, was caught on camera outside Number 18 High Street in Burwell sometime in the 1930s.

Acknowledgments

Cambridgeshire Collection, Cambridge Central Library
Christopher Jakes

Thanks are also due to
Peggy Burns who penned the editorial text and
Margaret Wakefield and Andrew Mitchell for their copywriting skills